Praise for Violence in Families

"Drawing on the deepest Christian values proscribing loving and respectful relationships, Reverend Al Miles weaves together personal stories, a clear analysis, and the courage to confront hard truths to help us understand and respond effectively to the scourge of family violence. An excellent resource, *Violence in Families* offers hope, practical advice, and a call to action for all Christians, lay people and clergy, survivors and perpetrators, teens and adults."

—Paul Kivel, violence prevention educator and author of *Men's Work: How to Stop the Violence That Tears Our Lives Apart*

"*Violence in Families* is one of the most informative books on domestic violence that I've read. Readers will be emotionally and intellectually engaged as Rev. Miles uses his experiences as a minister to challenge the invisibility of domestic violence in Christian families. Based on Christian principles, interpretations of the Bible, and stories told by Christian men, women, and teens, this book exposes misrepresentations of the Bible and Christ's teachings as they have been used to excuse abusive behavior. It explains a truly Christian understanding that the covenant of marriage is broken by abuse. Rev. Miles breaks new ground by recognizing that teenagers experience violence in dating relationships, and by providing excellent advice for teens and parents who face this problem. This is a valuable resource for Christian families, parents of teenagers, church leaders, and people of all ages who might be abusive or abused. It is filled with strategies for preventing and intervening to stop abuse in intimate relationships."

—Barrie Levy, clinical social worker, author of *In Love and In Danger*, *Dating Violence*, and *What Parents Need to Know about Dating Violence*

"Like the prophets of old, Al Miles does not hesitate to tell the truth about a very ugly reality that infects all of our churches. As a chaplain in a large city hospital, he has seen all too clearly the devastating effects of spousal abuse on Christian homes and communities. He not only exposes but also counsels, offering God's people paths of prevention, intervention, and protection."

—Catherine Clark Kroeger, Gordon-Conwell Theological Seminary; co-author, *No Place for Abuse*; co-editor, *Women, Abuse, and the Bible* and *Healing the Hurting*

"Domestic violence is an epidemic health and faith issue that the Christian churches have not fully understood. Al Miles makes accessible the stories of survivors of domestic violence, their cries for justice, and an analysis of the causes of violence. The churches must do more than condemn violence; we must organize and support prevention and healing programs. This book has the information every lay and clergy leader needs for understanding and action, and we urgently need to act for the salvation of the church as well as the safety of every person in United States' society."

—James Newton Poling, Ph.D., professor of pastoral theology, care, and counseling, Garrett-Evangelical Theological Seminary, Evanston, Ill.; author of *The Abuse of Power* and *Deliver Us from Evil;* minister and counselor

"Rev. Miles' second book breaks through layers of denial, exposes the truth that domestic violence occurs in Christian homes, and invites the church and individual Christians to take an honest look at domestic violence in their faith communities. He reveals what domestic violence experts have recognized for years: the wrong response to victims of domestic violence from the church can be worse than no response at all. *Violence in Families* offers information on how Christians can make the church a safe place for victims of domestic violence to seek help, while lovingly holding perpetrators responsible for their illegal and immoral behavior."

—Carol C. Lee, executive director, Hawaii State Coalition against Domestic Violence

"*Violence in Families* provides the Christian laity with a clear, no-nonsense exploration of domestic violence from the perspective of the individual Christian and the Christian church. The book also provides an excellent exposition of the concept of forgiveness and how forgiveness differs from reconciliation. Rev. Miles challenges and invites Christian congregations to develop solutions to end domestic violence both within their congregations and their respective communities. He cautions, however, that churches must collaborate with the broader community of domestic violence experts in order to be effective. This book will be an excellent addition for any Christian church lay library."

—L. Kevin Hamberger, Ph.D., professor of family and community medicine, The Medical College of Wisconsin; co-editor, *Treating Men Who Batter, Domestic Partner Abuse,* and *Violence Issues for Healthcare Educators and Providers*

Violence in Families

What Every Christian Needs to Know

Reverend Al Miles

Foreword by Marie M. Fortune

Augsburg Books
MINNEAPOLIS

This book is dedicated to my wife, Kathy. After more than thirty years of teaching me how to be free from abusive and violent behavior when I relate to other people and myself, I am amazed by how much she still has to offer—and by how much I've still yet to learn. I also dedicate this book to Dr. James Earl Massey. Three decades ago, this biblical scholar and father figure prophesied that one day I would need him even more than I needed him at the time. "One day" has arrived.

Scripture passages marked NIV are from The Holy Bible, New International Version, copyright © 1973, 1978, 1984 by International Bible Society. Used by permission of Zondervan Publishing House. All rights reserved.

Scripture passages, unless otherwise marked, are from the New Revised Standard Version of the Bible, copyright © 1989 by the Division of Christian Education of the National Council of the Churches of Christ in the USA. Used by permission. All rights reserved.

Large-quantity purchases or custom editions of this book are available at a discount from the publisher. For more information, contact the sales department at Augsburg Fortress, Publishers, 1-800-328-4648, or write to: Sales Director, Augsburg Fortress, Publishers, P.O. Box 1209, Minneapolis, MN 55440-1209.

Cover and book design by Michelle L. N. Cook
Author photo taken by Kathy Miles
Cover photo is of Tina Croucher. Please see pages 84-87 for her story.

Library of Congress Cataloging-in-Publication Data
Miles, Al, 1951–
   Violence in families: what every Christian needs to know / Al Miles.
   p.cm.
   Includes bibliographical references (p.).
   ISBN 0-8066-4264-5 (alk. paper)
   1. Church work with problem families. 2. Family violence—Religious aspects—Christianity. I. Title.
   BV4438.5 .M545 2002
   261.8'327—dc21   2002018613

The paper used in this publication meets the minimum requirements of American National Standard for Information Sciences—Permanence of Paper for Printed Library Materials, ANSI Z329.48-1984. ♾ ™

Manufactured in the U.S.A.   ▪

06   05   04   03   02   1   2   3   4   5   6   7   8   9   10

Contents

Author's Acknowledgments

One of the central themes of this book is that Christians, both clergy and lay members, can accomplish much when they work with each other and with service providers in the secular community. Teamwork is essential if we are effectively to prevent or intervene in situations of adult intimate partner abuse and teen dating and teen relationship violence. Otherwise, neither survivors nor perpetrators will receive all the help they need.

The people who graciously provided their expertise and time to the development of this book embody the collaborative spirit necessary when addressing such a complicated issue as intimate partner abuse. I thank Jesus Christ for all these individuals. I also thank Jesus Christ for keeping me balanced and focused. I am sometimes tempted to deal with everything in a single day—or in one book.

It's difficult to put into words the numerous contributions of my wife, Kathy. I especially appreciate her patience and understanding, which helped me feel less guilty during those weekends I spent researching and writing this book. Kathy read every single draft of my handwritten notes, even those drafts with little or no sentence structure. She typed and retyped the manuscript and, as has always been the case, was my strongest critic and my greatest supporter.

Appreciation must also be extended to the staff of Augsburg Books for the opportunity to publish my work with such a fine organization. Their editorial suggestions strengthen my points. I must single out one staff member, Michelle L. N. Cook. She has been the editor and designer of both my books. *Mahalo nui,* Michelle, for your excellent work. The same gratitude must be offered to my longtime personal editor, Victoria A. Rebeck. As always, her skills helped to clarify and enliven my thoughts.

A host of other people were invaluable throughout the project. They read the manuscript, made insightful comments, suggested people to interview, and assisted in many other practical and scholarly ways. *Mahalo nui* to Barbara Chandler, Bryant Chandler, Jeffery Chandler, Niki Christiansen, Nelda Rhoades Clarke, Diana Davids, Curtiss Paul DeYoung, Marie M. Fortune, L. Kevin Hamberger, Anne Marie Hunter, the staff of The California Interval House Domestic Violence Program, Kim Smith King, Catherine Clark Kroeger, Barrie Levy, Mimi Lind, the staff of Logos Productions, Inc., Julie Mall, James Earl Massey, Suzan Morrissette, Nancy Nason-Clark, Roy Prigge, William A. Smith, Carolyn Staats, Stephanie Thomson-Dick, and the staff of Zaferia Shalom Zone Agency.

Last, I have special appreciation for the survivors of adult intimate partner abuse and teen dating and teen relationship violence who tell their stories in this book, and also for the parents of the two young victimized women who were murdered by former boyfriends. Without their courage and trust, this project could not have been completed. *Mahalo nui* for sharing your stories with the world.

Foreword

It is a fact that victims and perpetrators of domestic violence are sitting in most churches in the United States every Sunday morning. This raises an important question: What are victims hearing and experiencing from their pastors and congregations, and how does this shape their efforts to deal with the experience of abuse?

Some victims are experiencing profound silence. They have never heard a word about spousal abuse or domestic violence spoken from the pulpit, in Sunday school, or at the congregational life committee meeting. They might draw one of two conclusions from this: either violence in their home is unique to them and never happens to other Christians, or their church just doesn't want to get involved in these messy, private situations. Needless to say, neither conclusion will do much to help them end the violence. Sadly, someone could end up dead.

Other victims and abusers are hearing sermons or classes encouraging the subordination of women in marriage and the headship of men over their wives and families. Although these supposed biblical teachings may not actually cause domestic violence, they certainly do support an abuser's justification of using whatever means necessary to control his wife and children. And for a victim of abuse, the teaching of subordination in marriage traps her in a secret, silent place in which questioning her abusive husband's treatment of her is blasphemous. (True blasphemy occurs when a teaching that was intended for good is distorted and misused to bring suffering and death.) She is likely to suffer in silence for years on end believing that his abuse is simply her "cross to bear."

Some church leaders have begun to question these dangerous teachings. The Catholic Bishops of Canada have stated that the church must take responsibility for the abuse of women when it has directed abused women to remain in relationships with batterers and when it has taught women's subordination in marriage. The bishops of Northern Canada were unequivocal: "Violence against women is profoundly wrong and is unworthy of human beings. It is a serious social problem. It is a crime. It breaks the fifth commandment and is a sin. Some people have taken passages from the Bible and used them to support abusive, violent behavior toward their wives. We reject this false interpretation of the Bible."

Hopefully some victims and abusers are now hearing this very different message. Hopefully victims are receiving a Gospel message that "you will know the truth, and the truth will make you free" (John 8:32), and that Jesus came so that we all might know abundance of life (John 10:10). Abusers might be hearing a word of confrontation: the prophet Malachi (2:13-16) says that God hates covering one's garment with violence and being faithless to one's wife. In other words, violence in a marriage is infidelity. The prophet Ezekiel (18:31) calls sinners to repentance: " . . . get yourselves a new heart and a new spirit!" And the message for both victim and abuser puts forgiveness into context: "If another disciple sins, you must rebuke the offender, and *if* there is repentance, you must forgive" (Luke 17:3, emphasis added). Forgiveness then becomes the last step, not the first.

If we begin to bring these liberating words to more and more of our churches, the response won't initially be one of gratitude. My colleague Dr. Rebecca Parker discovered this when she began to preach on domestic violence and sexual assault from the pulpit. The women's Bible class the next month was awkwardly quiet. One of the women spoke up and said that they had discussed it and they wanted Rebecca to stop preaching about these things that happen to women. Surprised, Rebecca asked why. All of the women burst into tears and their stories came tumbling out. She realized that her preaching had now made their silent suffering uncomfortable. They talked some more. "Do you really want me to help you keep silent?" Rebecca asked. As they shared their lives, their compassion for one another took over. Finally they said, "We think you should keep preaching about what really happens to women."

Our job as faithful Christians in response to domestic violence is threefold:

• We must help a victim of violence be safe. This begins with our willingness as friend or pastor to hear her story and realize the danger that she and her children may be facing. Then we can help her find the resources in our communities—from battered women's shelters to the police—that are designed to keep her safe.

• Secondly, we must help to hold the abuser accountable, legally and otherwise. Domestic violence is a crime and our criminal justice system, even with all of its foibles, is one means by which the community makes it clear that domestic violence is unacceptable. But there are other forms of accountability. The pastor and congregation can make it clear to the abuser that repentance—real change—is necessary. We will walk with an abuser on the road to repentance but we will not collude in his choice to continue to control and exploit his family.

• Finally, we must support the restoration of a relationship based on two conditions: the goals of safety and accountability must be accomplished *and* the battered woman must freely choose to attempt to heal the relationship, trusting that she is safe and that her abuser has truly repented. If these conditions are not met, then there is no relationship left to restore; there is no family to keep together. With his violence, the abuser has destroyed the relationship. Then it is our job to help the survivor and her children mourn this loss and move on in their lives.

With this book, Al Miles is giving us Christians a valuable resource. He is holding up a mirror to our churches and, through the voices of women, young and old, he is helping to tell the truth. A pastor friend of mine used to paraphrase the Gospel and say, "You will know the truth *and the truth will make you flinch* before it sets you free." This is surely the case for the church and domestic violence. None of us wants to hear the pain and suffering and so we allow one another to suffer silently and alone. Books like this one give us a chance, even when we flinch, to help the church be the church. Don't miss this opportunity.

In many rural communities in the 1970s, it was churchwomen who formed the first safehome networks providing safe, temporary shelter for battered women. It has often been churchpeople who have served on boards and raised funds for local crisis programs. And sometimes it has been local clergy who have led the effort to maintain social services, advocacy, and legal responses to domestic violence. Reverend Miles takes us one step further, showing congregations how they can respond with a solid foundation of awareness and a clear commitment to action. "Let anyone who has an ear listen to what the Spirit is saying to the churches" (Revelation 2:29).

—The Rev. Dr. Marie M. Fortune
The Center for the Prevention
of Sexual and Domestic Violence
Seattle, Washington

Preface:
Agents of Healing

A divine appointment. It had to be. I had no intention of attending a seminar on domestic violence. Why should I? After all, this issue didn't affect me. My world hadn't been touched by such things. But everything was about to change.

I had planned to attend a session on "Spiritual Growth through Journaling," scheduled at the same time. Both workshops were part of the continuing education offered at the International Convention of the Church of God in Anderson, Indiana. My workshop was cancelled, and I somehow made my way to a session on domestic violence. I found myself seated in a student desk in a classroom at Anderson University. I wasn't comfortable. I didn't know the first thing about abuse. Why was I there?

And then Rachel entered. No doors opened for her. There was no pomp and circumstance. Rachel was introduced to us through a series of pictures: a young, dark-haired woman in front of a Christmas tree. Smiling. Happy. Carefree, it seemed. The pictures showed Rachel and her family; Rachel and her friends. We were told to think about our feelings as we looked at these photos. Then the clincher came. The seminar leader, the Reverend Al Miles, explained that Rachel Boer was a victim of domestic violence and had been murdered by her boyfriend.

How could I have known that these pictures of a young woman, someone like me, would etch themselves into my memory? How could I have known that the life and, more specifically, the death of this young woman would profoundly affect me? God had made an appointment for me, and there I encountered Rachel.

I was not unlike many people who erroneously assume that if domestic violence has not yet affected my life, it never will. I was not unlike many Christians who erroneously assume that because our congregations' members speak about serving God, they would never commit acts of abuse and violence. I was not unlike many church professionals working in middle-class congregations who erroneously assume that domestic violence occurs only among the very poor or the very rich. By learning more about domestic violence, primarily through the work of Rev. Miles, I realized my assumptions were very harmful and potentially deadly.

My introduction to Rachel started my journey of learning about domestic violence. The embarrassing part of this personal journey was that I was so ignorant of the topic; even worse, I didn't realize the degree of my ignorance. As my knowledge increased, I understood that at any moment a victim of domestic abuse could enter my life. Statistics show that perpetrators and victims are more than likely sitting in the pews of my church. Any one of the young people I work with could be affected, directly or indirectly, by domestic violence.

My realization raised questions for me: What will I do about it? How can I sensitize myself to the needs of domestic abuse victims?

How can I use my position to educate young people and their parents about the realities of domestic violence?

After reading both *Domestic Violence: What Every Pastor Needs to Know* and *Violence in Families: What Every Christian Needs to Know,* I realized that as a young Christian woman and youth pastor I have a lot to learn about domestic violence before I am really ready to deal with this large and pervasive problem. Yet Al Miles's work has helped me to see ways in which I can become a part of the solution instead of allowing my ignorance to perpetuate the problem. I have begun to recognize the role each of us can play in the drama of domestic abuse.

Even with my limited understanding, I have learned how I can become an agent of healing for domestic violence victims. I've learned that the way I respond to victims can affect their ability to heal over the long run. *Violence in Families* lays out, clearly and concisely, appropriate and inappropriate responses to the perpetrators and victims of domestic violence. Readers will learn to avoid common mistakes when working with a victim or perpetrator.

Reading this book has raised another question for me: Now that I understand the role I can play in situations of domestic violence, will I have the courage to follow through?

I can never go back to knowing nothing about domestic violence and my obligation to become informed about it. Ignorance of domestic violence kept my ministry and my understanding of the tenets of my faith neatly wrapped in nice boxes of easy answers. No more. With one look at the photos of Rachel Boer, the face of domestic violence became personal. Rachel could very well have been my high school friend. She could have been my sister. She could have been me. Even more to the point, she could have been one of the young people to whom I minister as youth pastor. Part of my responsibility is to handle situations that arise among the youth of my congregation. This book gives me a starting place for educating myself, youth, and parents about abuse. It provides knowledge that gives me the courage I need to follow through.

God is the author and source of healing, and chooses to use each of us to administer tangibly the words and actions that can bring healing. We all have the potential to be healing agents in situations of domestic violence. If you have the courage to read this book, you will be challenged to change your assumptions, your outlook, and your behavior—especially if you are a Christian. I have no choice but to continue to educate myself. I cannot in good conscience, especially as a Christian, turn my back on what I have learned and live in the ignorance I once enjoyed. My prayer is that this book will move you to resolve to be an agent of healing in the midst of painful circumstances.

—Niki Christiansen, Youth Pastor
West Court Street Church of God
Flint, Michigan

Introduction: "There's No Place Like Home!"

We had climbed more than two thousand feet, my godson and I, to reach a sunny plateau overlooking a crater lake and snowcapped peaks. It was a gorgeous July day in the Colorado Rockies. Soon I'd be interviewing this young man, whom I had known and loved all his life. I was eager to hear his feelings and thoughts on growing up male and hoped to use them in a book I was writing. In the valley far below us, my wife strolled in peaceful solitude, attempting to capture on film the incomparably beautiful surroundings. "Betcha she really misses this place," my godson surmised. He knew my wife had grown up in Colorado. "Yep, she sure does," I replied. "As they say 'There's no place like home!'"

Dorothy's line from *The Wizard of Oz* had no real bearing on the sacred time I was having with my godson. We did the interview for the book and then rejoined the rest of the family for the long hike back down the mountain. It was only after I completed the main body of this book that I began to recognize a disturbing irony in the often-quoted line from that classic movie. For many women and children, "home" is not a safe haven, but a place where they are frequently beaten, cursed, raped, and terrorized in other ways.

Taking part in a panel discussion at an international conference in San Diego on family violence, I was deeply troubled by the solemn truth spoken by another panelist, the Rev. Dr. Marie Fortune, a pioneer in domestic violence awareness. She called home "the most dangerous place for women to live and for children to grow up." Unfortunately, her statement is supported by national statistics. According to the American Medical Association, nearly one-quarter of all women in the United States—more than twelve million—will be abused by a current or former partner some time during their lives.[1] By the sheer numbers alone, this mind-boggling figure should alert people of faith to another shocking truth: "home" is also an unsafe place for many Christian women and their children.

Wherever I travel in the United States to conduct domestic violence awareness trainings with clergy and congregation members, invariably a host of young and older women disclose tales of the horrors they suffered from Christian husbands and boyfriends. The survivors reveal that their oppressive situations are exacerbated by the refusal of their spiritual leaders and other members of their congregations to believe the survivors' disclosures of abuse. Or, the survivors are told that they themselves are to blame for their own suffering.

The five chapters of this book provide several documented cases, told by Christian survivors, of how clergy and laity offered inappropriate and at times downright cruel responses to the victims' cries for help. However, these brave women and teenage girls don't just point out how so many of us let them down spiritually and emotionally. These survivors also offer Christians redemption: If we admit that intimate partner abuse and teen relationship violence occur even among our neighbors and those sitting next to us in church on Sunday morning, and if we will seek the necessary education and training in domestic violence prevention and intervention, then they, the survivors, will gladly help us learn how to be effective and sensitive caregivers. It's an offer no concerned Christian can afford to decline.

There's no place like home! Leslie, Kim, Sandy, Anita, Janine, Gladys, Margaret, Christie, Carol, Lani, Paula, Lorena, and Brenda share with us the ironic pain in the truth of this statement for so many women and teenage girls. Rachel and Tina, whose voices have been silenced, also offer their stories to us. Their souls still cry out for justice, and they continue to teach us invaluable lessons.

Let us Christian clergy and lay people open our eyes, hearts, and souls and receive the many teachings offered by these courageous victims and survivors. They are our mothers, children, sisters, friends, neighbors, and parishioners, and we have the responsibility to help them find places of safety and wholeness that, for them, were never part of the place called "home."

1.

A Dim Mirror: Hidden Dynamics of Domestic Violence among Christians

Picture the following three women attending the same church where you worship: Rose, a fifty-eight-year-old homemaker, is the most dedicated person in her congregation—the individual everyone counts on. Everyone affectionately calls her "Mom." Outgoing and nurturing, Rose gives freely of her money, talent, and time. Carla, age twenty-eight, has been attending worship services for the past six months. Never one to draw attention to herself, she sits alone every Sunday morning in an out-of-the-way spot near the back of the sanctuary. Her smile is warm, but always brief. She respectfully declines all invitations to church functions like dinners, picnics, or study groups. After worship Carla hurries home, seldom stopping in the narthex to receive a greeting from anyone. Stacy is seventeen and the pride and joy of the entire parish. She's an honor student, a youth leader, and a volunteer helper of elderly and infirm persons. In a month she'll be attending the most esteemed university in the state on a full academic scholarship. Everyone is convinced that one day Stacy will return home to practice medicine in the community. In addition to being Christians who attend the same congregation, Rose, Carla, and Stacy have at least one other thing in common: each is a victim of intimate partner abuse.

Christian women (and Christian teenage girls) are no less vulnerable to domestic violence than are females from the general public. One of every four women in the United States is abused by an intimate or former intimate partner.[1] It may be difficult for some churchgoers to accept, but this statistic alone suggests that there are both victims (whom I will also refer to as "survivors") and perpetrators of domestic violence worshiping in every congregation. Many Christians deny the sad reality that some men and boys who "praise Jesus" on Sunday mornings abuse their wives and girlfriends the rest of the week. Hidden securely behind the ornate stained glass windows, and buried deep within the hearts of many people seated in the pews of churches across the United States, incidents of domestic violence flourish like a fire raging out of control.

Consider the story of a survivor named Leslie. Born and raised in a Christian family, this fifty-seven-year-old woman endured, for eleven years, a hellish marriage to an abusive Christian man named Ted, the son of an ordained minister.

Leslie's Story

"Ted and I both grew up in strict religious households," recalls Leslie, looking back on a relationship that began more than forty years ago. "Our families allowed no drinking, smoking, going to movies, card playing, and absolutely no activities on Sundays except for attending church." Leslie was sixteen when she began dating Ted, who was eighteen. The courtship seemed normal. "I wouldn't say Ted was attentive," she says, "but he was nice. We took long drives and communicated well together. Ted certainly seemed smitten with me, and I thought he was a person I could trust. There was no indication he was an abuser, at least not when we were dating."

Within two weeks after they were married, however, Leslie began to realize that Ted had some serious problems. "My husband came home for supper after work and then would leave the house, with no explanation, and not return until three in the morning, drunk. I now realize he was an alcoholic." Leslie asked Ted where he went every night, and he'd always reply with an onslaught of vile words. "Ted would shout, 'You have no right to question me, bitch! Who the hell do you think you are? I can do whatever the hell I want, you dumb cunt!' I couldn't believe such cruelty was coming out of the mouth of the man who supposedly loved me— a Christian man at that."

Ted began to physically abuse Leslie a few weeks later. He would slap her across the face, punch her in the stomach, and throw her on the floor or against a wall. Ted's verbal attacks also continued. "I never knew what was going to set him off," Leslie says. "At first I thought the violence was happening because Ted was a drunk. But soon I discovered he was just as abusive while sober. I was constantly walking on eggshells, trying desperately to appease my husband. But nothing worked. Ted's violence persisted, and it quickly escalated."

After nearly every attack, Leslie's husband expressed remorse and promised never to hit her again. He also bought her expensive gifts. "Ted would always cry, apologize profusely for abusing me, and then he'd buy me all kinds of items on credit we couldn't afford. Eventually we went bankrupt because we were unable to pay the bills when they came due." Feeling trapped, Leslie finally decided to turn for help from Brenda, another woman in the parish and the wife of one of the church elders. "Brenda seemed like a very compassionate person," Leslie says. "She listened intently as I told her all about Ted's problems with alcohol and how he was abusing me physically and verbally. I don't remember

Brenda saying much, but I certainly felt comforted by her. I was an eighteen-year-old woman in my first year of marriage to a Christian man who said he loved me. Yet he was doing all these nasty things no Christian husband should have been doing to his wife. I felt unloved by Ted, and even by God. So I poured out my heart to Brenda, a sister in the Lord, whom I thought was loving and trustworthy."

Leslie soon discovered the elder's wife did not keep confidences. A few days after listening to Leslie's disclosure, Brenda repeated her story to Ted's mother and father, the congregation's pastors. "To my in-laws, Ted was a fair-haired child who could do no wrong," Leslie says. "They were in total denial of their son's alcoholism and simply refused to believe that he was also a wife beater." Confronting her daughter-in-law at home early one morning, Ted's mother made it clear she thought Leslie was either lying about Ted's behavior or was to blame for it. "I'll never forget that terrible day," Leslie says. "Ted and I were having breakfast when his mother stormed into our tiny apartment and verbally attacked me. 'I understand you told a bunch of lies to the wife of one of our church leaders,' she shouted. 'You claim that my precious son is an alcoholic and a wife beater. My husband and I both know this couldn't be further from the truth. Ted is a wonderful Christian son and, we are certain, a loving Christian husband to you. How dare you spread such lies! Even if any aspect of the story is true, you must have driven him to drink and hit you. You should get on your hands and knees and beg Ted's forgiveness.'" Leslie remembers that Ted said nothing the entire time his mother was unleashing her verbal barrage. "He had this smug look on his face as if to say, 'You tell her, Mother!'" After her mother-in-law left the apartment, Leslie got down on her hands and knees and asked Ted to forgive her. "After that incident, I never talked to another soul about my husband's abuse," Leslie says. "I knew I couldn't trust anyone in the church, and God seemed like a distant figure who didn't care in the least about me. So I just suffered alone."

What Exactly Is Domestic Violence?

Domestic violence is a pattern of abusive behavior in which a person uses coercion, deception, harassment, humiliation, manipulation, and/or force in order to establish and maintain power and control over that person's intimate partner or former intimate partner. Perpetrators use economic, emotional, psychological, physical, sexual, spiritual, and/or verbal tactics to get their way. (These tactics are discussed in detail on pages 35-36.) Domestic violence is the number one public health problem for women in the United States. According to the United States Surgeon General, domestic violence is the greatest single cause of injury among U.S. women, accounting for more emergency room visits than traffic accidents, muggings, and rape combined.[2] While a small percentage of men are also violated (which is discussed on pages 32-33), the American Medical Association estimates that two million women in this country are assaulted by an intimate partner every year.[3] The actual numbers are probably much higher because victims often do not report attacks, fearing both the stigma associated with abuse and the threat of reprisal from perpetrators. In addition, a report published in July 2000 by the Justice Department's National Institute of Justice and the Department of Health and Human Services' Centers for Disease Control and Prevention states that nearly twenty-five percent of surveyed women say they have been raped and/or physically assaulted by a current or former spouse or partner at some time in their lives.[4] And these alarming statistics do not include many of the emotional, psychological, and spiritual tactics male perpetrators use to abuse their female victims.

Are Christian men, because of their faith, less likely to abuse? Are Christian women who are victims guilty of provoking their husbands or boyfriends, through actions or inactions, to use violence against them? Why do so many Christian victims of spousal abuse remain married to their violent husbands? Let us carefully consider these frequently asked questions, dispelling along the way commonly held myths and stereotypes.

Victimized Women: Never the Cause, Often the Blame

At the beginning of sessions I lead on domestic violence awareness, I pass around photographs of a young Christian woman named Rachel Leah Boer. A beautiful white woman, this twenty-four-year-old native of Oskaloosa, Iowa, was shot to death by a former boyfriend in 1997, five days before Christmas.[5]

I ask conference participants, most of whom are clergy and lay leaders in churches, to study the photographs carefully. I ask them to think of Rachel not as a stranger, but as their own daughter, granddaughter, niece, sister, friend, next-door neighbor, or beloved church member. I then ask that they focus on their feelings (rather than make assumptions). In small groups, participants discuss what they feel after learning of Rachel's murder. Most people quickly divert from the stated assignment and respond in one of two ways. Many participants, especially those who are white, say that Rachel could not possibly be a victim of domestic violence. They insist Rachel is too young and too beautiful and is less vulnerable to the problem because she's a Christian and from a small town. Many of them say that because Rachel is white, it is "highly unlikely" she would ever "put herself in such a dangerous situation."

Many others suggest that Rachel is at least partially to blame for her own murder. They say:

- Rachel made a bad choice in a partner.
- She must have come from a dysfunctional family.
- Rachel had to have liked being abused.
- She looks like a free-spirited, independent woman seeking trouble.
- Are you sure Rachel grew up in a Christian home?

When asked why they chose to make comments about Rachel (rather than follow the assignment to discuss their feelings), many gradually admit it is much easier to "focus on Rachel." They acknowledge that they want to distance themselves from the horrors of domestic violence in general and, especially, Rachel's tragic death. A number of women express fear that they, too, could be violated by a husband or boyfriend. (Some women, after concentrating on their own feelings, become aware they are already being victimized!) And women and men alike slowly face the harsh realization that all females—including the women and girls in their own churches, communities, and families—are vulnerable to becoming victims of abusive male partners.

Rachel Leah Boer's experience teaches lessons about victims of domestic violence that no Christian can afford to minimize or ignore. Although it may be difficult to believe and frightening to accept, women of all ages, cultures, races, socioeconomic levels, and religions (including Christianity) are equally vulnerable to attacks by their current or former intimate male partners. (In my position as a hospital chaplain, most of the domestic violence victims I have counseled are employed as educators, nurses, physicians, psychologists, social workers, and pastors.) The terror inflicted upon them has nothing to do with their having done a poor job in choosing a mate, being "drawn" to abusive men, having been raised in dysfunctional families, and/or provoking men to violence. These myths and stereotypes add to the isolation and devastation victimized women are already facing. Batterers, and batterers alone, are responsible for the abuse and violence they perpetrate.

Why Christian Victims Stay

Nevertheless, one of the most frequently asked questions about victims of domestic violence is why so many of the women choose to remain with men who violate them. (Curiously, people seldom ask why so many men, even Christian men, abuse the women they claim to love.) Many factors lead victimized women to stay with abusive men. A few of them are:

• Isolation from family, friends, places of worship, and community resources.
• The perpetrator's promises that he will change.

• The perpetrator's threats to kill, kidnap, or physically harm the victim's children, parents, siblings, pets, and the victim herself, or to kill himself. (Caution: All threats made by perpetrators must be taken seriously. The most dangerous time for a victimized woman, by far, is when she attempts to leave her abusive partner.)

• The victim loves her abuser. (Most women don't want their marriages or partnerships to end. They want the abuse to stop.)

• The batterer and others blame the victim for the abuse and she is told it's her responsibility to fix the problem.

Yet another factor keeps victimized women who are Christians in dangerous relationships: religious beliefs, teachings, and traditions. In the next chapter, we'll look at how religious beliefs have been both a resource and a roadblock for women of faith seeking relief from abuse. Now, let's listen to victimized Christian women themselves describe why they remained with abusive husbands and boyfriends. (Keep in mind that most of the male batterers discussed in this book identify themselves as Christians.) All the stories told by survivors throughout the book are true. In some instances, the women's names have been changed and certain aspects of their stories have been altered to protect their anonymity and safety.

> There is no doubt in my mind or heart: I stayed married to my abusive husband because of the Christian convictions I held at the time. Then I believed that nothing happened outside of God's control, that every situation we faced in life was part of God's plan for us and served God's purpose. My understanding of God led me to believe that God willed me to be in an abusive marriage.
>
> —KIM SMITH KING, ORDAINED MINISTER IN THE PRESBYTERIAN CHURCH (U.S.A.). REMAINED MARRIED TO HER ABUSIVE HUSBAND FOR NINE YEARS.

> In those days, after I accepted the Lord, I thought it was my duty to stay with my husband, no matter how severe his abuse became. I felt that was what the Lord would want a Christian wife to do: to stay with her husband no matter what, no matter how bad it got.
>
> —LESLIE, HOMEMAKER. REMAINED MARRIED TO HER ABUSIVE HUSBAND FOR ELEVEN YEARS UNTIL HIS DEATH.

I stayed married because my self-esteem was pretty low after years of emotional and verbal put-downs from my husband. There really wasn't much physical abuse. However, he'd call me all sorts of terrible names: "whore," "fatso," "banana boobs," because I'm not very big on my chest, and he'd tear down my looks and how I walked. His abuse really worked against me. I didn't like myself very much, and I felt like I wasn't good to anybody. I certainly wasn't happy in my marriage. But because of my low self-esteem, I told myself this was probably the best man I could get.

—SANDY, ADVOCATE FOR DOMESTIC VIOLENCE VICTIMS. REMAINED MARRIED TO HER ABUSIVE HUSBAND FOR NINE YEARS.

I thought it was my Christian duty to stay with my husband. He was manipulative, charming, charismatic, and could win people to the Lord. He was a walking civil war—wanting to be godly, but he couldn't believe that God loved him as he was. I convinced myself I could save him, and that our staying together was good for the church and our children—even though he abused them too. Divorce was just not in my vocabulary. I thought it was my Christian duty to remain with my husband.

—ANITA, ORDAINED MINISTER. REMAINED MARRIED TO HER ABUSIVE HUSBAND FOR TWENTY-THREE YEARS UNTIL HIS DEATH.

I stayed because I was pregnant. Also, I grew up with both my parents in the home. So I couldn't imagine my children not having both parents there. Another reason I stayed was because in my Christian upbringing divorce was wrong, no matter what was taking place in the marriage. Divorce was breaking a vow I'd made with God, my church taught. In addition, I couldn't admit to myself that I'd gotten into something I couldn't handle and that somehow I had failed. You know, I didn't want anybody to know that I had gotten in over my head and there was nothing I could do, no matter how hard I prayed, to make my husband treat me right.

—JANINE LIMAS, COMMUNITY EDUCATION DIRECTOR FOR CALIFORNIA'S INTERVAL HOUSE, A DOMESTIC VIOLENCE PROGRAM. REMAINED MARRIED TO HER ABUSIVE HUSBAND FOR SIX YEARS.

The church I grew up in taught if a husband is not physically abusive, then a wife needs to stay married to him. Everything will be okay, I was told. But what has really got me thinking about leaving is my husband's constant emotional abuse. The effects of that last a whole lot longer than the physical stuff. As a child of God, I now know that God does not want me to be abused in any way. My plans are to leave my husband, but it's going *to have to be in secret. I don't think it's safe for me to come out and tell my husband about my plans.*

—GLADYS, WHITE-COLLAR PROFESSIONAL. CURRENTLY LIVING WITH
HER ABUSIVE HUSBAND OF SEVERAL YEARS.

Male Victims

"What about all the men being abused by their wives and girl-friends?" This question is raised at nearly every domestic violence awareness training I facilitate—and always by male participants. "Women are just as likely to victimize their intimate partners as are men," I am constantly told. While leading a half-day domestic violence awareness training seminar on Oahu for seventy-five ordained and lay ministers, five very angry men approached me during one of the breaks. "You need to give a more balanced point of view," demanded one clergy member. He was reacting to my keynote address, in which I said that although anyone can be a victim of intimate partner abuse, women are far more likely to be violated than men. "I hear stories all the time of men living in hell because of their abusive wives," the spiritual leader continued. "We're not the only ones who perpetrate," he barked. "Women do it, too!"

Yes, there are male victims of domestic violence, in both heterosexual and homosexual intimate partnerships. And no matter the gender of the perpetrator, abuse is wrong. But, when looking at what motivates women to resort to violence, we must keep in mind self-defense. Women most often turn to using violence against their husbands or boyfriends after living for years under the physical, psychological, and sexual torment of these men. Sometimes women turn to violence in efforts to protect their children when the men begin to abuse the victims' children.

"Women are more adversely affected by intimate partner violence than are men in a variety of areas: injury rates, injury severity, medical help seeking, depression, anxiety, fear," write researchers L. Kevin Hamberger and Clare Guse in a paper addressing what abusive men say about their partners' violence. "In addition, recent research has indicated that while some women report using violence to dominate and control their partners, the predominant violence motivation offered by women is self-defense or retaliation for prior violence against them."[6]

When it comes to the sin of domestic violence, facts do not support a "balanced point of view" that asserts that women perpetrate violence against their intimate partners as often as men do. Although some men are victimized by their intimate female partners (and, in homosexual relationships, by their male partners), the vast majority of victims are women. And, in most instances, perpetrators of domestic violence are men.

As we next look at the various dynamics associated with male perpetrators, it is important to keep in mind the following two nouns: deceit and manipulation.

Male Perpetrators: Slick, Not Sick

Simply put, one of the primary reasons men have violated women throughout history is that church and society have allowed them to do so. Even now, at the start of the twenty-first century, far too few communities hold men accountable for their violent behavior against women. This is especially true within the religious world. As we'll see in chapter 2, the religious community has generally refrained from holding men responsible for the domestic violence they perpetrate. Religious groups are likely either to look the other way or to blame females for their own victimization. As in society in general, many people of faith continue to excuse male violence, especially toward women, as either some sort of inbred (but acceptable) character flaw, or as actions that are ordained by God. And when a churchgoing man is accused of abusive or violent behavior, many people in the Christian community refuse to believe it could be possible. Take note of a few reactions I've heard from Christian leaders and laity in various parts of the United States after they learned about male churchgoers who were accused of perpetrating acts of domestic violence against their wives:

- I've known him for years. There's no way this fine man of God would ever rape his wife.

- Like all of us, he's a sinner saved by grace. His wife needs to be more understanding of his shortcomings.

- Yes, he broke many of the bones in his wife's body, and she was in the hospital for several weeks. Still, she has to realize his God-given authority and must submit to him in all things.

- He called her a few nasty names. So what? It's not like he beat her. Satan must have had a hold on him.

- His wife had to have done something to provoke his anger. Besides, I think the night he beat her he had a little too much to drink.

Christians need to recognize that women are not responsible for men's abuse and violence against them; they do not "cause" or "provoke" it. Also, we need to understand that the abuse is not caused by alcohol, drugs, children, job stress, pets, or Satan. Men use abusive and violent tactics (discussed on pages 35-36) because these tactics are very effective at getting them what they want, when they want it, and because they know that, for the most part, society will not hold them accountable for it.

"Violence is very functional for men who batter," explains Dr. L. Kevin Hamberger, a Christian and clinical psychologist on the faculty of the Medical College of Wisconsin Family Practice Residency Program, in Racine, Wisconsin. Since 1983, his primary work has been conducting treatment and research with men who batter their wives and girlfriends. Hamberger dispels the myth that domestic violence has to do with men having problems controlling their anger. "The abuse rarely relates to intense anger or with a man having problems managing his anger," he states. "It has much more to do with a batterer thinking, 'I use violence because it works. I'll do whatever is necessary to keep this person under my control.'"

Most perpetrators are slick, not sick. Although some have a diagnosable mental illness, the vast majority do not. Further, though the number one predictor for determining if a boy is more likely to become a man who abuses is whether that boy witnessed his own mother being abused, some perpetrators grew up in loving and non-violent homes. Men who batter women come from all cultures, races, religions (including Christianity), and socioeconomic levels. They live in rural, urban, and suburban areas, and can be unemployed or work as actors, athletes, attorneys, construction workers, educators, law enforcement officers, physicians, psychologists, social workers, clergy and other pastoral ministers, and in all other fields.

Tactics

Perpetrators of domestic violence use various assaultive behaviors to coerce their victims to do what they want, when they want. It is important for Christian leaders and church members to remember that these inappropriate actions have nothing to do with victimized women: not with what the women say, not with what they do, not with how much the women weigh, nor with how the women dress, cook, parent, handle finances, or respond sexually. Perpetrators, and perpetrators alone, are responsible for their criminal and sinful behavior. Here are some of the assaultive behaviors used by batterers:
- physical: hitting, punching, slapping, use of weapons, etc.
- sexual: pressured or coerced sex, forced sex
- psychological:
    1. Threats of violence against victim, self, or others
    2. Acts of violence against self or people other than victim
    3. Attacks against property or pets
    4. Emotional abuse, humiliation, degradation
    5. Isolation of victim
    6. Use of children (threats to take them away, etc.)
    7. Threats of deportation
- economic coercion[7]

Another tactic male batterers use against their female intimate partners is *spiritual abuse*. This form of domestic violence is especially damaging to Christian women and their dependent children. Spiritual abuse is characterized by the use of God; Jesus Christ; Scripture; the batterer's position as clergy, deacon, pastoral minister, or lay leader; religious beliefs; teachings; and traditions to support physical, emotional, psychological, and sexual battering. (We'll discuss this in greater detail in chapter 2.) Spiritual abuse is sometimes employed by men who would never set foot in a church or any other religious institution. Most frequently it is practiced by males who identify themselves as Christians.

"My position as a pastor played a huge part in the privilege I was enjoying," admits Rev. Mark-Peter Lundquist, a former batterer who abused his wife for several years, all the while serving as parish pastor. Although he claims never to have used physical force, Lundquist says he always knew exactly what impact his behavior, and his position as a faith leader, had on his wife emotionally, psychologically, and spiritually. "I would throw things and punch walls," the minister confesses. "My actions were all geared around explosive and rageful outbursts to get her to do what I wanted. The message I was communicating to my wife was clear: 'If I can throw newspapers or a chair, and if I can punch walls, think of what I can do to your body. So you better do whatever I say.' I knew my behavior was wrong, but I knew also I could get away with it because I am a male and also a clergy person."

Perpetrators of domestic violence cannot be identified by their appearance. One of the many myths about male abusers is that they have a certain "look." Although victimized women speak often about the "look" their batterers have prior to and during an attack, out in public most abusers look and act like all other men. In addition, the "look" battered women talk about is often secret, known only to them and their perpetrators.

In my experience, Christians are especially vulnerable to the deceitful and manipulative practices of perpetrators in two areas. First, many of us believe that no "man of God" would ever use violence and other abuse tactics to control his wife or girlfriend.

Second, a lot of Christians are fooled by an abuser's claim of being a "man changed by God." Let us separate the two concepts in order to better illustrate the dangerous aspects of each.

"No man of God would ever use abuse and violence against his wife or girlfriend"

For thirteen years, a woman named Arlene endured emotional and physical abuse from her husband, Robert, an ordained deacon in their church.

"Robert was a master manipulator," Arlene says. "He had a real gift of finding out both the strengths and weaknesses of other people, and then using them to his advantage."

Arlene gives the example of a man named Michael. He was the Catholic priest who served as pastor at the church she and Robert attended. "Father Michael loved desserts and wine," Arlene explains. "Somehow, within a matter of a few weeks, Robert was able to discover the exact sweets and vintage our priest preferred. Robert then began showering Father Michael with expensive Swiss chocolates and fine French wines. As a result, the priest viewed my husband with high regard. 'Robert is a dream parishioner,' Father often professed. This made it very difficult, I think, for him to remain neutral when I finally disclosed some of the episodes of abuse Robert had been perpetrating against me for years."

According to Arlene, her husband was a little boy living in a man's body. "Like a spoiled kid left alone in a candy store, Robert was used to getting what he wanted whenever he wanted it," she says. "Whether it was fancy sports cars, a new set of expensive golf clubs, or sex, my husband's desires were all that mattered to him." When Arlene didn't consent immediately to Robert's demands, he would throw a temper tantrum. He'd call her vile names and would also accuse her of not being a "loving Christian wife" because she wasn't willing to "please" him. This manipulative ploy nearly always worked. "I felt guilty for not being a better wife to my husband," Arlene says. "So, usually, I'd end up giving him whatever he was demanding at the time."

However, there were times that Arlene said she refused to give in. It was then that Robert began using physical force to get his way.

Arlene says that, initially, her husband focused his physical outbursts on objects. "He'd punch walls, kick doors, and occasionally break a few dishes." But, over time, Robert started battering Arlene as well. "My husband broke many of the bones in my body, gave me several concussions and punctured eardrums, and he left more black and blue marks on me than I care to remember," Arlene says. "This self-proclaimed 'man of God' never once took responsibility for the violence he perpetrated. Instead, he'd tell me I was to blame for the abuse. 'If you'd only submit to my will,' he'd shout, 'then I wouldn't have to discipline you.' What real man of God would actually discipline his wife or treat her in such cruel ways?" Depressed and demoralized, Arlene finally turned to her priest for help. But the priest's response made matters worse.

"Father Michael had always been loving to both my husband and me," Arlene says. "However, when I told him about all the degrading ways Robert had treated me over the years, the first phrase out of the priest's mouth was, 'You must be mistaken.' He then proceeded to tell me that no Christian man, especially one with Robert's moral character, would ever treat his wife in the terrible ways I described. So, in my minister's eyes, I guess I was a liar."[8]

The voices of other Christian women and how they were treated by their "men of God" further illustrate the hidden dynamics of domestic violence among churchgoers.

> He'd grab my breast in front of other people and say "I have a license to do that." I got into the habit of laughing when I was embarrassed. I told my husband I was uncomfortable with this behavior, but he continued to do it. He'd even grab my crotch in public. He'd tell people I was insatiable and tell them also about certain sexual acts I liked. He'd even say these things to teenage boys. And he would stare, point at, and comment about teenage girls, those in our church youth group and in the general public. My husband always liked pornography, too. He wanted me to perform acts that I did not feel comfortable doing.
> —ANITA, ORDAINED CHRISTIAN MINISTER. MARRIED TWENTY-THREE YEARS TO AN ABUSIVE CHRISTIAN MAN WHO WAS ALSO AN ORDAINED PASTOR.

My husband used his power in abusive ways in his attempt to control me. He would try to isolate me from other people, monitoring my phone conversations, limiting my ability to leave the house, or prohibiting me from inviting others into our home. On one occasion he grabbed the phone from my hands, at another time he ripped the phone from the wall. He sought to control my actions and monitor my every movement. For example, I had to turn in receipts for everything I spent, down to the penny. If I parked at a meter on the street and spent a quarter, I had to turn in a receipt. Of course, parking meters don't issue receipts, so he would berate me for not being able to produce paperwork that would account for every single cent spent. He was also verbally abusive, calling me names including "stupid" and "slut." One of my most painful memories is of the time he taught our three-year-old son to say, "Mommy is a slut." My husband laughed with glee when he got our son to repeat the phrase.

—KIM SMITH KING, ORDAINED MINISTER IN THE PRESBYTERIAN CHURCH (U.S.A.). MARRIED NINE YEARS TO AN ABUSIVE CHRISTIAN MAN.

If my husband didn't like what I cooked, he'd throw the food and plate against the wall. If he didn't like the way I ironed his shirts, he'd just rip all the buttons off and throw the shirt on the floor. Then he'd scream profanities, calling me a "dumb cunt," "fucking bitch," "stupid," and whatever else came to his mind. I felt so worthless as a Christian, as a wife, and as a woman.

—LESLIE, HOMEMAKER. MARRIED ELEVEN YEARS TO AN ABUSIVE CHRISTIAN MAN.

My husband used mostly emotional and verbal abuse against me. If he didn't get his way, he would yell and scream and rant and rave. He'd talk about how I was a "bitch," that I was "fucking insane," "fucking crazy," that kind of stuff. And he would leave without telling me where he was going. He'd be gone all night, maybe come home the next day, but he wouldn't talk with me for several days. Then he'd start acting normal after that, never discussing where he had been, what he had been doing, and never discussing his abusive behavior. It would be like "let's pretend that it never happened, that everything between us is okay." And we'd go on from there.

—MARGARET, BUSINESSWOMAN. MARRIED FIVE YEARS TO AN ABUSIVE CHRISTIAN MAN.

As people of faith, we must recognize a sad and ugly part of Christian life: there are men who sit in the pews of our congregations, who teach in our Sunday school classes, who serve on our boards, who sing in our choirs, and who speak from our pulpits who also beat, cuss, rape, and violate their wives and girlfriends.

"I am a man changed by God"

I stood silently in front of the 125 workshop participants, most of whom were Christian clergy and lay leaders. Shaking my head in disgust, I crossed my arms tightly against my chest. We were moments away from concluding an all-day domestic violence conference. For nearly eight hours, the group and I had talked about the various aspects of adult intimate partner abuse and how these dynamics affect people of faith. Much of the morning we had discussed the slick and manipulative behavior of male perpetrators. One minute the perpetrators will abuse their wives and girlfriends, I explained, and the next they'll shower them with affection, kind words, chocolates, diamonds, flowers, and empty promises. Many perpetrators, following an attack on their intimate partners, will beg for forgiveness, I said, and also quickly declare themselves to be a "man changed by God." But the acts of loving kindness and claims of spiritual conversion are false, I cautioned. These are more tactics a perpetrator uses to maintain control over his victim and to get what he wants.

Despite the great amount of time we spent talking about this, many of the workshop participants were captivated by the words of a male attendee who, at the end of the conference, leapt suddenly to the podium and demanded to give his testimony. "I used to beat and abuse my girlfriends in various ways," the man confessed in a tone fit for a revival service. "But now God has changed me. God has made me a new man." Even though he offered no context by which the alleged changes had occurred, and though most of the attendees with whom I spoke afterwards admitted they did not personally know this man, several pastors and lay leaders responded to his claim of being a man changed by God with applause and with affirming religious intonations: "Amen," "Glory be to God," "Praise the Lord," "Preach, Brother."

I strongly believe that anyone can be changed by the power of God. However, achieving healthy and lasting change usually requires a difficult and long-term process. Those of us who have struggled with keeping our weight down, for instance, know that it's much easier to lose pounds than to keep them off in the long run. Former cigarette smokers and alcohol and drug users hang onto the credo "One day at a time" to help them in their struggle to break free permanently from these behaviors. Men who abuse their intimate partners find that their path to lasting change is even more demanding.

Although I firmly believe that these men can change, I also know that they must commit themselves to a long-term effort. From a Christian viewpoint, this means several things. A vital first step is repentance—showing remorse for our sins, taking full responsibility for the damage we've caused others, and being willing to work on correcting any inappropriate behavior so that we won't repeat our harmful actions.[9] True repentance means a complete 180-degree turn from previous behavior. And it is often the case that such repentance may need to occur on a daily basis.

We Christians must not be fooled by the claims from an abusive man who says he is "changed by God." (Or, as was the case at the workshop I just described, be too quick to accept and affirm the testimony of an admitted batterer about whom we know little or nothing.) We must be especially wary if the alleged divinely inspired change occurs over a short period of time, if the man shows little or no remorse for the damage he's caused, if the man attempts in any way to blame anyone or anything other than himself for the abuse, or if the man refuses to seek (or stay in) a batterers' intervention program. (Remember, domestic violence has little to do with a man having problems managing his anger. Therefore, referring a perpetrator to an anger management program will not help him stop his abusive behavior.) If an abuser is not willing to commit himself to the difficult and long-term process required to affect lasting change, then he will never truly become a man "changed by God." (We will discuss the necessary steps needed for abusive men and boys to change in chapter 4.)

Effects of Domestic Violence on Children

One of the many myths about domestic violence is that it has little effect upon children who grow up in an abusive home. Even adult female survivors have said to me that they believe it fortunate that all the times their partners abused them happened when their children were either asleep or out of the house. However, the children who grew up in homes where abuse occurred—and experts who work with kids who witness or experience firsthand domestic abuse—tell a much different story.

Christie Corpuz's Story

During my hour-long interview with her, twenty-six-year-old Christie Corpuz is composed. Clear and concise, her words belie her subtle smile. Moments after the tape recorder is turned off, however, things abruptly change. Christie begins to cough violently. Her eyes quickly water, and her smile has given way to desperate gasping for air. "I have a really nervous stomach," Christie explained after thirty minutes of this distress. "It's because of all that."

The "all that" is Christie's past. She was the oldest child of parents who were both faithful churchgoers. Her father was the congregation's men's ministry president and in charge of church administration. But at home, Christie witnessed and experienced firsthand the horrors of abuse that her dad perpetrated. "I always knew something [in our home] wasn't right because there was always tension in my parents' relationship," Christie says. "As far back as I can recall, I have memories of Daddy abusing Mom. He'd call her 'stupid,' 'bitch,' 'whore,' and 'the perfect asshole.' In the same breath, he'd tell her that 'nobody will ever love you the way I love you.' Mind you, my father was a self-proclaimed 'man of God,' one of the leaders of our church. But that didn't stop him from abusing my mother in all kinds of ways—or from sexually abusing me when I was three, which he continued to do for many years."

Seeing her father violate her mother and suffering from his abuse firsthand affected Christie profoundly. "As a child growing up I thought abuse was normal," she explains. "Anybody who didn't live in a home with violence, I told myself, must be from a weird family." But, over the years, Christie says she began to realize how much growing up in an abusive home has hurt her. "I still live with a sense of impending doom. I try to avoid conflict because I fear it will always turn violent. I'm still very nervous if I'm out walking somewhere, constantly fearing I'll be attacked." Christie also admits she has a difficult time with intimacy and an intense distrust of most men.

Plagued by recurring nightmares, Christie gets very little sleep. "I can't remember exactly what the dreams are about, but I know there's a lot of blood and a lot of darkness. Somebody is hurting me, and I can even feel the pain. So I don't sleep well, averaging only two hours per night. As a result, I'm always tired."

Having experienced "salvation" at age six, Christie has always had Christian faith as a central part of her world. But, she says, the abuse she witnessed and suffered from her father has had a negative impact upon this sacred part of her existence. "At age twelve, someone prophesied that God had given me the gift of music," she tells me. "When my brothers and I would sing, members of the church often cried because they felt ministered to by us. But Daddy would say 'See, you sang so badly that you made people cry. I don't even know how you can stand in front of the church in the first place; everybody knows what a slut you are. You're a whore and are going to hell.' These awful words were coming out of the mouth of a Christian man, my father, the same person who was constantly abusing my mother and me. What a hypocrite!"

Christie's father's words and actions severely damaged her faith. "As a result of what Daddy said and did to me, and seeing how he treated my mother, I thought that God was somebody else's God," Christie laments. "He was certainly not my God—even though he was omnipotent and omnipresent, my mother and I kept being abused by my father. I would often plead, 'God, if you're all good things, why aren't you stopping all the bad things my father is doing? Why, God, aren't you sending your angels to protect us? Why all this pain and suffering?' Eventually, and for a long period of time, I completely lost my faith in God."

According to the Massachusetts Department of Youth Services, children who witness violence in their home are:
- six times more likely to commit suicide
- twenty-four times more likely to commit sexual assault
- fifty percent more likely to abuse drugs and alcohol
- seventy-four percent more likely to commit crimes against others[10]

Devastating. That's how Allana Wade Coffee describes the effects of domestic violence upon children who witness or experience the problem firsthand. A clinical therapist who works in the mental health department at Kaiser Permanente in Honolulu, Coffee has counseled children and their parents for years. She talked about the sensitive nature of children and how they respond to even the normal, healthy arguments of their parents. "After I became a mother and my husband and I so much as raised our voices—what most people would call a normal argument between parents—my children became silent, withdrawn, and eventually angry," Coffee observes. "And this was in response to a regular argument. So imagine what it must be like for children who witness violence in the home. Though it's been many years, my heart still breaks when I think about one particular child I interviewed. The child told me, 'I watched my dad break my mom's jaw,' 'I watched my dad throw my mom down the stairs,' 'I watched my dad rape my mom.' I think of this child all the time."

Coffee says in her experience one of the worst effects on children who witness domestic violence is their lack of trust. "It's a blanket—these children don't trust adults," she says. "Whether this means that they become defiant and oppositional with teachers or other people of authority, or they just stop talking, the fact that children lose trust and a sense of safety with their caregivers is very bad." Coffee acknowledges this lack of trust also means that these children will probably not seek help from adults should they get into trouble.

Another common effect on children who witness or experience domestic violence is *cognitive distortion.* Coffee explains: "One common misunderstanding children will get from growing up in homes where abuse is present is a lot of black-and-white thinking. Somebody is the perpetrator and somebody is the victim. There's a good person and there's a dangerous person. There's a wrong person and a right person. This sort of dichotomous thinking is one example of a cognitive distortion."

Coffee cites as an example a child being referred by a teacher to the principal's office for a disciplinary problem. "If this particular child is from a home where violence is present," she says, "he or she will put the experience through a distorted filter. The teacher will be seen as either a person on their side or a person not on their side. These children don't have any shades of gray; their thinking is very black and white. So, when I try to do any kind of counseling or mediating or reality testing with them, they are on one side or the other. It's hard for me to initiate the 'what if' conversation, because they've already made up their mind."

Children who witness and experience domestic violence first-hand are also at high risk for being involved in abusive relationships during their teen and adult years. In chapter 3, we discuss this issue more fully. But it is important to note two items here. First, not all children who grow up in abusive homes become victims or perpetrators. Second, some victims and perpetrators have grown up in nonviolent and loving homes. Therefore, Christians must resist the temptation to predict which children will or will not later be involved personally with the problem of domestic violence.

How Christians Can Help Victims and Perpetrators

Christian clergy and laity can take a very important role in the care of both victims and perpetrators of domestic violence. However, it is vital for us to remember this is an extremely complicated issue requiring professionals and laity from both the religious and secular communities. We must never work with victims or perpetrators alone, or go beyond our level of training and expertise. Here are ways Christians can more effectively help victims and perpetrators:

Make the safety of a victim and her children top priority. This is a vital first step. (As we will see in the next chapter, far too many Christian clergy and laity still consider the top priority to be the sanctity of the marriage covenant. This greatly concerns me.)

Listen to and believe a victim's story. Always thank a victim for the courage and trust she demonstrates by sharing her story with you. Tell her that there is no excuse or justification for domestic violence. Refrain from asking for more details about the abuse than what a victim volunteers (especially if you are a male and the victim has experienced any form of sexual assault). Also, never ask a victim what took her so long to disclose the abuse or why she stays with her abuser. These questions could seem to a survivor like she is being blamed for her own victimization. Special caution: Never bring a victim together with her batterer to discuss episodes of abuse or suggest she and her perpetrator seek couples' counseling.

Do not recommend couples' or marriage counseling. It is a common, but dangerous, mistake to suggest that a battered woman and her partner or husband seek couples' or marriage counseling. Domestic violence is *not* about men and women struggling as a couple. It *is* about the decision of one partner, usually the male, to use abusive and violent tactics to maintain power and control over his female intimate partner. Couples' or marriage counseling is inappropriate and risky, and it could lead to further abuse and even death.

Seek education and training. If Christians are to play a vital part in helping a victim and perpetrator of domestic violence, then it is essential that we seek proper and ongoing education and training. We must keep updated on the articles, books, videos, and workshops that can help us become effective team members. Remember, even with this training, never try to care for a victim or batterer alone. (The Center for the Prevention of Sexual and Domestic Violence in Seattle has excellent educational resources for religious leaders and laity. The organization can be reached by phone at 206-634-1903, or on the Internet at www.cpsdv.org.)

Establish a safety plan for the victim. Christian clergy and laity can assist a victim of abuse by helping her establish a safety plan that can be implemented quickly should her husband's or boyfriend's abuse continue or escalate. Include in this plan a safety kit, kept in a place where the perpetrator will not discover it, that contains items such as cash, a change of clothing, toiletries, an extra photo identification card, and a list of phone numbers of counselors, friends, pastors, and shelters.[11] It bears repeating: although Christians can offer vital assistance to a victim in the area of safety planning, remember that we must work with a team of community service providers to provide a victim with the best possible opportunities for safety. (An invaluable resource for creating a safety plan is the guidebook *Striving to be . . . Violence Free* published by Perspectives. For more information call 952-926-2600.)

Hold an abuser accountable. Remember, a perpetrator of domestic violence is deceitful and manipulative. He rarely takes responsibility for his destructive behavior, blaming instead alcohol, children, drugs, job stress, mood swings, Satan, and, especially, his victim.[12] While it is important for Christians to affirm the love, forgiveness, and healing that Christ offers, it is vital that we not get taken in by an abuser's slick and manipulative ways. We must also resist the notion that no self-professed "man of God" would use violence and other forms of abuse to control his wife or girlfriend, and be very leery of a perpetrator's quick and unrealistic claim of being a man "changed by God." Remember to refer an abuser to a batterers' intervention program rather than attempting to provide this complicated type of care yourself.

Law enforcement officials and members of the criminal justice system also have a key role in holding batterers accountable for the abuse they perpetrate. Jail time and/or ordering an offender into mandated counseling, for example, might deter perpetrators. But, as with members of the church and the rest of society, there is still a widespread tendency in the law enforcement community to blame victims for intimate partner abuse. As psychologist Neil Jacobson and John Gottman write in their book *When Men Batter Women,* the blaming can affect the relationship between domestic violence and the criminal justice system:

• It can prejudice law enforcement officials against the wives, thus making it less likely that laws will be enforced.

• It can reduce support from family and friends, thus isolating the battered woman further and ultimately making her *more* dependent on her battering husband, and therefore more likely to stay in the relationship.

• It can lead prosecutors not to seek indictments against batterers, because they assume that battered women will not press charges or will eventually drop them.[13]

Domestic Violence Affects Human Beings

Even though it is mind-boggling to cite statistics detailing the overwhelming amount of abuse perpetrated by men against women in the United States, it's still too easy for clergy and other Christians to dismiss or minimize these situations. Statistics in and of themselves are not personal enough.[14] It helps to remain aware at all times that domestic violence affects *human beings*.

For years, I let statistics about domestic violence victims and perpetrators go in one ear and out the other. These numbers did little to compel me to actively work against domestic violence in my role as a Christian leader and concerned citizen. Then one day I heard the story of a young Christian domestic abuse victim named Carol.

By her own admission, Carol had not grown up in an abusive home. "My parents loved each other. They never physically fought, and my father would never dream of hitting my mother," Carol says. "In fact, I can remember Daddy saying, 'Before I'd hit your mother, I'd leave the house.' He had a wonderful habit of walking away when he thought he would say or do something to Mama that he would later regret." From her mother, Carol received a strong message to avoid physically abusive men. "Mama said countless times to my sister and me, 'If a man hits you once, he'll hit you again.' So I made up my mind to never get into that type of situation. I even coined a slogan for all women: 'Don't get used to abuse.'"

Despite this upbringing, one night Carol found herself in a hospital emergency room being treated for a broken jaw and other injuries inflicted by her boyfriend. "I felt so much shame," Carol says. "My parents raised me better than that. And I felt more ashamed when the woman doctor treating me said, 'You're going to keep going back until you get your brains beat out.' Also, I kept hearing my Mama's voice saying, 'If he hits you once, he'll hit you again.' So I knew I had to get out of that relationship."

This survivor's story forced me to change my indifferent attitude toward victims of domestic violence, for Carol is my younger sister.

Christian clergy and laity must always view victims and perpetrators of domestic violence as our sisters and brothers, sons and daughters, nieces and nephews, friends and neighbors, and individuals who worship with us in church, for that is who they are.

Conclusion

Hidden deep within the community of believers worshiping in churches around the globe is an ugly secret: domestic violence occurs among Christian couples just as it does among couples in every other corner of society. There are men who identify themselves as followers of Jesus Christ who beat, curse, rape, and violate their wives and girlfriends. There are Christian women (and their children) who live not in God's peace, but under the constant horror of being tortured emotionally, physically, psychologically, and sexually by males calling themselves "men of God."

Domestic violence among Christian couples will not disappear or lessen if we continue to deny its existence or blame women for their own victimization. Women in no way ask for or cause men to violate them. One of the primary reasons so many men assault their female intimate partners with impunity is that, in both the religious and secular worlds, we do not hold men accountable for their inappropriate actions.

If Christians are to help victims and perpetrators of domestic violence, we must first acknowledge that the problem exists among us. Second, we must seek ongoing education and training in domestic violence intervention. Third, we must work collaboratively with service providers within our communities, while also always being aware of how much we can help and the point at which we need to rely on others for assistance.

Questions for Discussion

1. Describe your reaction to Leslie's story, told on pages 24-26. Are there victims of domestic violence worshiping at your church? If you answer no, tell why you think this epidemic is not present in your congregation. If you answer yes, how are church members caring for battered women?
2. Name at least five reasons victims stay with their abusive partners.

3. Are there perpetrators worshiping at your church? If you answer no, explain why. If you answer yes, discuss how members of the congregation are dealing with the men. (Reminder: male perpetrators *are* in most congregations.)
4. What are the necessary steps for a batterer to become truly a "man changed by God"?
5. List at least five ways children are affected when they either witness or experience firsthand domestic violence.
6. As a result of reading this chapter, how will you now care for victims and perpetrators worshiping among you?

2.

In the Name of God and Jesus? Religious Beliefs, Teachings, and Traditions That Work against Battered Women

Throughout history men have used religious beliefs, teachings, and traditions to justify their violation of women and children. But this spiritual abuse tactic has not been limited to use by batterers alone. Clergy and congregants from all the major religions have also misinterpreted and mistranslated holy texts and doctrine to support male dominance and female subjugation. The practice continues to this day.

The patriarchal system has certainly always been alive and well in Christianity. Both the Hebrew Bible and Christian Scriptures have an androcentric, or male-centered, perspective and emerge from patriarchal societies. Some texts, which actually are misogynist (women-hating), are lifted up to the exclusion of other texts that clearly affirm mutual respect between the sexes. Still other texts have been twisted—inadvertently *and* intentionally—to suggest that our loving and merciful God and Jesus Christ for some reason grant males authority and privilege over females. Because of all the above, men have received special dispensation from Christian clergy and laity alike to do whatever they desire with their wives, girlfriends, daughters, and all other females, without any fear of accountability. Take note of what church fathers have said about women through the ages.

> You are the Devil's Gateway. It is you who plucked the fruit of the forbidden tree. You are the first who deserted the divine law. You are the one who persuaded him whom even the Devil was not strong enough to attack. All too easily you destroyed the image of God, man. Because of your desert, that is death, even the Son of God had to die. . . . Therefore cover your head and your figure with sackcloth and ashes. (Tertullian [160-225 C.E.])[1]

> Why must a woman cover her head? Because, as I explained before, the woman does not possess the image of God in herself, but only when taken together with the male who is her head, so that the whole substance is one image. But when she is assigned the role as helpmate, a function that pertains to her alone, then she is not the image of God. But as far as the man is concerned, he is by himself alone the image of God, just as fully and completely as when he and the woman are joined together into one. (Augustine [354-430 C.E.])[2]

> As the philosopher says, "Woman is a misbegotten male." Yet it is necessary that woman was made in the first production of things as a helpmate. Not indeed as a helpmate in any other works than procreation, for in all other works man can be more efficiently helped by another man than by a woman, but as a helper in the work of generation. . . . The woman is in a state of subjugation in the original order of things. For this reason she cannot represent headship in society or in the Church. Only the male can represent Christ. For this reason it was necessary that Christ be incarnated as a male. It follows, therefore, that she cannot receive the sign of Holy Orders. (Thomas Aquinas [1225-1274 C.E.])[3]

When a woman thinks alone she thinks evil, for the woman was made from the crooked rib which is bent in the contrary direction from the man. Woman conspired constantly against spiritual good. Her very name, femina, means "absence of faith." She is insatiable lust by nature. Because of this lust she consorts even with Devils. It is for this reason that women are especially prone to the crime of witchcraft, from which men have been preserved by the maleness of Christ. (*Malleus Maleficarum* [fifteenth-century manual of the Dominican Inquisitors against witches])[4]

Eve originally was more equally a partner with Adam, but because of sin the present woman is [a] far inferior creature. Because she is responsible for the Fall, woman is in a state of subjugation. The man rules the home and the world, wages war and tills the soil. The woman is like a nail driven into the wall, she sits at home. (Martin Luther [1483-1546 C.E.])[5]

The covenant of creation dictates a certain order, a relation of priority and posteriority, of A and B. Just as God rules over creation in the covenant of creation, so man rules over woman. He must be A; he must be first. She is B; she must be second. He must stay in his place. She must stay in hers. She must accept this order as the right nature of things through which she is saved, *even if she is abused and wronged by the man*. (Karl Barth [1886-1968 C.E.]. Emphasis added.)[6]

It is the unbroken tradition of the Catholic Church that women have never been admitted to Holy Orders, with which the Orthodox tradition also concurs. Jesus Christ did not call any woman to be part of the twelve, even his own mother. The apostolic Church faithfully carried out this exclusion of women from priesthood that was instituted by Christ. Moreover, it should also be said that the maleness of the priest reflects the sacramental mystery of Christ and the Church. As representative of the Head of the Church, the bridegroom, the priest must be male. There must be a "natural resemblance" between the priest and Christ. For Christ himself was and remains a male. (Vatican Declaration on Women's Ordination, 1976)[7]

Are God and Jesus really the sexist bigots many Christians portray? Do the "divine beings" truly grant to men authority over women even when these men abuse their wives and girlfriends? And what about some of the religious beliefs, teachings, and traditions that are said to be "in the name of God and Jesus"? Are the issues that often get evoked when incidents of domestic violence occur among Christian couples—namely divorce, forgiveness, marriage covenant, male headship, female submission—actually being addressed by clergy and congregants in ways God and Jesus would condone?

This chapter will probe these questions. We'll use the Christian Scriptures as a primary reference, but we will look closely at a few of the Hebrew Bible passages that Christians frequently cite as well.

Let us begin by considering the story of William and Helen. Childhood sweethearts and highly successful university professors, the couple has been married for eighteen years. Helen and William are also both mature Christians, actively involved in their congregation for more than a quarter of a century.

Helen and William's Story [8]

"My husband first revealed a side of himself I'd not previously seen a week into our marriage," says Helen. "During our wedding night he told me that he 'requires' sex every night. I thought he was joking, but soon discovered he was dead serious."

The first time Helen declined her husband's lovemaking demand, a week into their marriage, he unraveled. Abruptly getting up out of their bed, William stormed out of the room and went downstairs to the kitchen. "I thought he was making himself a cup of tea because I heard water running into the kettle," Helen recalls.

William returned to the bedroom five minutes later, lifted the blanket off of his wife, who was starting to fall asleep, and poured scalding water all over her body. "I was so shocked and frightened by what he did that I didn't even feel the pain of my second-degree burns until later," Helen says. "As I lay in bed crying uncontrollably over what this man, my husband, had done to me, William put his face very close to mine and said in an angry but even tone, 'Never,

ever refuse to have sex with me again. I am your master, you are my servant just as the Bible says. I'll be damned if I let my wife tell me what she will and will not do.'"

The abuse that William still perpetrates against his wife became even more imprisoning and tortuous after their two children were born. Always accusing Helen of having an extramarital affair with any male—a checkout boy at the grocery store, service station attendants, and most of her male students—William misjudged his wife's maternal love for their children as a "further sign of marital infidelity." He told Helen that the Bible commanded him to "punish" her for being unfaithful. "William not only increased his physical and sexual abuse," Helen says, "but he also made me give away my beloved cat and birds. He then ordered me to cut off all outside relationships, even with my two sisters, and forced me to make up some lie about how I thought they'd stolen something from our home one Christmas. He also stripped me of all financial independence."

Even though she is a tenured professor, Helen has no line of credit. Several years ago, William closed all of the couple's joint accounts and put everything—cars, credit cards, checking and savings accounts, and their home—in his name. "I don't even have the means to use a credit card to charge a carton of milk or a can of soup," Helen says.

While Helen lives in a perpetual hell on earth, William flourishes. Last year he was honored in his town as both professor and community person of the year.

Even though William has constantly told his wife (and children) she would suffer the consequences should she ever leave him or tell anyone about his abuse, Helen says she's thought a lot lately about exposing her husband as "the fraud he's always been." But, the battered wife quickly adds, "William is loved by everyone at the university, in the community, and at church. Our pastors and the entire congregation view him as the perfect husband, father, and man of God. Who would even want to believe that he's an evil monster at home?"

This disturbing story clearly demonstrates how batterers (and others) traditionally use God, Jesus, and Scripture to justify the sinful and criminal acts men perpetrate against women. William's physical, psychological, sexual, and spiritual abuse of Helen is reprehensible and is not supported by any biblical teachings. Nevertheless, he boldly declares the Bible has given him authority to be the "master" of his "servant" wife. Further, the abusive husband claims Scripture instructs him to "punish" his wife for her alleged infidelity. Here again, in the Christian Scriptures, there are simply no passages that support William's contentions. In fact, as we'll see throughout this chapter, the Scriptures clearly condemn violence against women and children. The cornerstone of a healthy Christian marriage, we are told in several passages, is mutual love, mutual respect, and mutual humility between wives and husbands. Domestic violence is not loving, not respectful, and not humble. It is damaging, illegal, and sinful behavior.

Nevertheless, when an incident of adult intimate partner abuse is disclosed about a couple worshiping in a Christian congregation, the usual response from both clergy and parishioners is to blame the female victim, defend or excuse the behavior of the male perpetrator, and to then recite a long list of reasons why battered women need to remain with their abusive and dangerous husbands. Let us concern ourselves with five of the most frequently cited justifications offered by Christians: sanctity of marriage, sinful nature of divorce, "God-given" authority husbands have over their wives, "God-ordained" duty of wives to submit to the authority of their husbands, and the sacred virtue of forgiveness.

The Sanctity of Marriage

"A marriage must be saved at all costs." Christian clergy and congregants typically spout this statement in response to reports of domestic violence involving couples in their congregations. Oddly, the individual who is designated to be the marriage "savior," the person on whom all the responsibility falls to fix any problems associated with marital abuse, is usually the battered wife. "I was taught by my church and told by my father that, no matter what, commitment to one's marriage was the most important thing—especially for Christian wives," recalls Anita, an ordained minister who was married twenty-three years to her abusive husband, Leonard, also a clergy person.

Despite her husband's constant emotional, physical, psychological, sexual, and spiritual abuse, Anita says other Christians told her that it was her responsibility to stay with, pray for, and change Leonard and his inappropriate behavior. Anita accepted this. "It never once occurred to me to leave," Anita admits. "I was aware of Leonard's extramarital affairs—some even with teenage girls at the church where we were pastoring; aware of his use of pornography and the sickening fact he once had sex with a dog; aware that Leonard was at all times emotionally abusive with me; and I was aware that, during our entire twenty-three years of marriage, he never ever complimented me on anything. Still, it was my job as a Christian wife, many church members told me and I myself believed, to stay with my husband."

In Christian tradition, marriage between a woman and man is indeed a sacred covenant; an oath taken by two people before God and Christ usually in the presence of family, friends, and other well-wishers, to stay together until parted by death. As part of most Christian wedding ceremonies, the couple also vow to honor, love, respect, and be faithful and kind to one another. The apostle Paul comments on the holy and mysterious nature of this bond, and about the responsibilities of Christian husbands, in a letter written to all the Christian churches near the city of Ephesus. (We will look more closely at this particular section of Ephesians on pages 68-73 when dealing with the issue of male headship and female submission in a Christian marriage.) Paul writes:

Submit to one another out of reverence for Christ. Wives, submit to your husbands as to the Lord. For the husband is the head of the wife as Christ is the head of the church, his body, of which he is the Savior. Now as the church submits to Christ, so also wives should submit to their husbands in everything. Husbands, love your wives, just as Christ loved the church and gave himself up for her to make her holy, cleansing her by the washing with water through the word, and to present her to himself as a radiant church, without stain or wrinkle or any other blemish, but holy and blameless. In this same way, husbands ought to love their wives as their own bodies. He who loves his wife loves himself. After all, no one ever hated his own body, but he feeds and cares for it, just as Christ does the church— for we are members of his body. "For this reason a man will leave his father and mother and be united to his wife, and the two will become one flesh." This is a profound mystery—but I am talking about Christ and the church. However, each one of you also must love his wife as he loves himself, and the wife must respect her husband (Eph.5:21–33 NIV).

Situations of domestic violence clearly stand outside of Paul's admonishment to Christian husbands concerning how they must treat their wives. A husband needs to love his wife as he loves himself, as Christ loves the church. Domestic violence disregards Paul's instructions and disrespects Christ and his church. Abuse also causes a great amount of damage to wives, children, and, ultimately, to the batterers themselves because perpetrators miss out on the many blessings God offers husbands and wives when both individuals commit to the biblical virtues of love and respect. Domestic violence is neither loving nor respectful, and Christians must resist following the traditional path many churchgoers take of labeling all marriages between Christians as "holy."

Catherine Clark Kroeger and Nancy Nason-Clark comment on this all-too-familiar pattern in their book *No Place for Abuse:*

Glorifying marriage and prescribing rigid roles do not lead to healthy relationships. Rather, a concern for hurting families is more likely to lead to marriages that can be made whole. Within our churches there must be freedom to acknowledge problems and to seek the support of fellow Christians. When the silence is broken, God's people can address the problem. Energies can be directed to healing instead of hiding. The biblical pattern is not to conceal abuse but to bring it to light and seek solutions. Let us confess that we are the imperfect and sinful people of God. We cannot be a forgiven people until we have confessed our failures and sought restitution and healing. It's messy and costly and embarrassing. But God can work when there is honesty. Separation is not necessarily failure. It may be the path to something far better! God's purposes for the family are higher than ours.[9]

It is important for churchgoers to understand that not all marriages between Christians are holy; some are ruined by abusive actions. We must also realize that the Christian Scriptures do not support violence against women. On the contrary, many scriptural passages in both the Hebrew Bible and Christian texts strongly condemn acts of violence perpetrated against any human being:

> Do not envy the violent and do not choose any of their ways. (Prov. 3:31)

> Do not envy the wicked, nor desire to be with them; for their minds devise violence, and their lips talk of mischief. . . . Whoever plans to do evil will be called a mischief-maker. . . . If you faint in the day of adversity, your strength being small; if you hold back from rescuing those taken away to death, those who go staggering to the slaughter; if you say "Look, we did not know this"—does not [God] who weighs the heart perceive it? Does not [God] who keeps watch over your soul know it? And will [God] not repay all according to their deeds? (Prov. 24:1-2, 8, 10-12)

> A bishop, as God's steward, must be blameless . . . must not be arrogant or quick-tempered or addicted to wine or violent or greedy for gain; but must be hospitable, a lover of goodness, prudent, upright, devout, and self-controlled. (Tit. 1:7)

> My friends, if anyone is detected in a transgression, you who have received the Spirit should restore such a one in a spirit of gentleness.

Take care that you yourselves are not tempted. Bear one another's burdens, and in this way you will fulfill the law of Christ. (Gal. 6:1-2)

You have heard that it was said to those of ancient times, "You shall not murder"; and "whoever murders shall be liable to judgment." But I say to you that if you are angry with a brother or sister, you will be liable to judgment; and if you insult a brother or sister, you will be liable to the council; and if you say, "You fool," you will be liable to the hell of fire. (Mt. 5:21-23)

And the tongue is a fire. The tongue is placed among our members as a world of iniquity; it stains the whole body, sets on fire the cycle of nature, and is itself set on fire by hell. . . . With it we bless [God], and with it we curse those who are made in the likeness of God. From the same mouth come blessing and cursing. My brothers and sisters, this ought not to be so. (James 3:6, 9-10)[10]

The sanctity of the marriage covenant is broken by all sorts of sin, and spousal abuse certainly qualifies. The Rev. Dr. Marie M. Fortune, a noted pioneer in the study of domestic violence, writes:

We have always taught within the Christian tradition that the marriage covenant is broken by adultery or sexual unfaithfulness in marriage. The main reason that adultery is a problem is that it results in broken trust between husband and wife. If the promise is made to be monogamous, then adultery breaks that promise. But, we should also realize that there are other kinds of unfaithfulness. Bringing violence into one's marriage is also unfaithfulness. Once violence has entered a relationship, trust is destroyed. If you can't trust your husband not to hit you, what can you trust?[11]

Despite the abusive behavior perpetrated by some husbands who call themselves Christians, many victimized women of faith are either told outright by pastors and other churchgoers—or infer the message—that they must keep their marriages and families together and that it is primarily their responsibility to do so. Listen to the voices of Christian survivors:

I'm still very confused about my faith. I feel like I really was trying to be a good Christian woman. Yet I was abused by both my brother and by my so-called Christian husband. And when I decided to divorce my husband, my church and family disowned me. They acted as though everything that happened was my fault, as though I was a bad Christian.

—LANI, HEALTHCARE PROFESSIONAL, MARRIED TO AN ABUSIVE CHRISTIAN MAN FOR NINE YEARS.

I was taught at home and church to "turn the other cheek" as many times as was necessary. I guess I thought of God as a God of punishment. No matter what we had to go through as his children, the church taught me, we probably deserved it. So the message I got from my church was it would be a grave sin to run from an abusive marriage.

—LESLIE, HOMEMAKER, MARRIED TO AN ABUSIVE CHRISTIAN MAN FOR ELEVEN YEARS.

I always felt like [the abuse] was my fault. I can remember really struggling with this, a struggle I still face daily. I had failed at being a good wife and at keeping my marriage together. I was raised in a Christian home and things such as domestic abuse were not supposed to happen to a Christian woman. At my church, marriage was always talked about as such a good thing. But what happens to women whose marriages fail because of abusive husbands? These women need to hear from pastors and other Christians that they're okay; that God still loves them.

—PAULA, CHRISTIAN EDUCATION DIRECTOR, MARRIED TO AN ABUSIVE MAN FOR FIFTEEN YEARS.

As Christians, we must never put the sanctity of a marriage covenant before the safety of a woman and her children. Instructing battered wives to remain with their abusive husbands is inappropriate, as it compels them to return to an extremely dangerous situation. Telling victims that God, Jesus, or the Bible demand that marriage is a sacred bond to be saved "at all costs," and that wives need to take responsibility for the spiritual, psychological, and emotional welfare of their battering husbands is also a misreading of Scripture and very risky for the victims of abuse. A marriage where domestic violence is present is not a sacred bond. It is an unhealthy and unsanctified union (damaged entirely by the perpetrator's behavior) that not only wounds but could also bring death to women and children.

Divorce as Sin

The beliefs of many Christians regarding divorce have caused problems for Christian women who are victimized by their husbands. The idea that marriage is a sacred covenant that must be "saved at all costs," coupled with the notion that divorce, under any circumstances, is a personal affront to God and Jesus, has kept many women of faith in dangerous relationships with violent men.

"Anything and nothing would trigger Paul's physical abuse," recalls Gladys, a longtime Christian and white-collar professional married several years to a man who also identifies himself as a Christian. "My husband was very careful while I was pregnant not to punch me in my stomach. He was also always careful to beat me where the bruises wouldn't show: on my back and, especially, on my legs. He'd use his fists, for sure, but his favorite weapon was a belt. He beat me nonstop."

Although Gladys says that Paul's physical battering ceased a few years ago, his psychological abuse continues to this day. "In the past, my husband's pattern was to curse and beat me physically, then he'd apologize profusely," Gladys explains. "This period of abuse was relatively short. But Paul's emotional and psychological battering goes on and on until he sees I'm at my breaking point."

Gladys told of a conversation she and Paul had one evening before supper. "That night we decided to talk and agreed it would be for only one hour," she remembers. "Actually, it ended up being a very good talk. Afterward, Paul asked me to sit on his lap. He wanted to be physically intimate. He wanted me to show him, both physically and sexually, that everything in our marriage was great because of this one-hour conversation. Talking was fine, but it certainly didn't erase all the years of abuse he'd perpetrated against me. I just didn't want to hold, kiss, or have sex with Paul. So I went to prepare dinner and we watched TV." Later that same evening, when they got into bed, Paul started a huge argument. "Paul proceeded to bring up past issues, like the death of my mother when I was four years old. And, the thing is, he knows how much this subject hurts me. Nevertheless, he harped on her death until I was bawling and begging him to stop. Paul started in on me because I had refused to have sex with him earlier that evening. Part of my husband's emotional and psychological abuse of me is his knowing what hurts me, and digging incessantly at that exposed nerve."

Seeking refuge from the pain her husband caused, Gladys decided to disclose Paul's abusive behavior to another Christian woman at her church. "It was a Wednesday. My friend asked if I would be attending the mid-week service a little later that night. I told her I didn't want to go and then began telling her in detail about Paul's emotional abuse of me.

"Then she asked if she might have prayer with me. I replied, 'Sure, you can pray that I get a divorce.' I thought I knew this particular woman well enough to be honest with her. But my friend shouted, 'I rebuke your suggestion. It's not like your husband is hitting you. Divorce is a sin, and I won't pray for you to take part in that!'" The response of Gladys's friend and others in that congregation left Gladys feeling trapped in an unhealthy marriage. "The message I always got from that church was that because Paul was no longer hitting me, I had no right to divorce him," Gladys says. "So I decided to stick out my marriage."

Even in cases where husbands beat their wives, many Christians believe and teach that divorce is wrong. Kim Smith King, now an ordained minister in the Presbyterian Church (U.S.A.), lived for nine years under emotional, physical, psychological, and spiritual abuse from her husband, who was also a professed Christian. When she attempted to separate from her husband, and later divorce him, he pointed to the biblical teachings on the wife being subject to her husband. He reminded her of her Christian duty to be under his authority. He argued that as a Christian she must stay married to him. He was joined in his efforts by his father and grandfather, both clergymen. All three men talked repeatedly of the sacredness of the covenant of marriage, the biblical prohibitions against divorce, and the "God-ordained" hierarchy that placed males over females and husbands as "lord" of their households.

What do the Scriptures actually teach about divorce? Are there any circumstances in which divorce is permissible? Why do so many Christians talk about the sinful nature of divorce, while so few discuss the sin of domestic violence? Let us look to Scripture to find answers to these questions.

A personal note: I have never once, not in all my twenty years of service as a Christian minister, counseled anyone—domestic violence victim, perpetrator, or anyone else—to get a divorce. I often make this confession at the domestic violence awareness trainings I lead for Christian clergy and laity. When I think I've captured the participants' attention, I offer a few follow-up statements. First, I say that one of the primary reasons I have never counseled a victim of domestic violence to seek a divorce is that ending the marriage will not ensure her or her children's safety. In fact, national statistics tell us that by far the most likely time a battered woman will be killed is when she tries to report abuse or leave the abuser. Divorce, then, greatly increases the chances that a woman will be harmed, rather that providing her safety.

Second, I don't tell a battered woman to get a divorce because I do not think it is proper for me to do so. I strongly believe that telling an abused woman to seek a divorce is just as inappropriate as telling her she should never seek a divorce. The decision to divorce or stay married must always be left up to the woman herself. Telling a victim what she can and cannot do in this matter (and others) creates yet another prison for her. In addition to being controlled by her husband, she is now controlled by her counselor.

Third, I say that although I do not tell victims of domestic violence to get divorces, I do encourage them to seek safety and empowerment for themselves and their children. A choice regarding divorce should never get in the way of what should be the primary goal of any domestic violence intervention: safety for victimized women and their children.

Fourth, regarding the personal decision to divorce, I believe that a battered woman has every right to choose it, according to the teachings of both the apostle Paul and Jesus Christ himself! The

Christian Scriptures offer two circumstances under which divorce is approved: "unchastity," which is rendered in some translations as "unfaithfulness" or "immorality," and on the grounds of desertion.

> But I say to you that anyone who divorces his wife, except on the grounds of unchastity, causes her to commit adultery; and whoever marries a divorced woman commits adultery. (Matthew 5:32)

> And I say to you, whoever divorces his wife, except for unchastity, and marries another commits adultery. (Matthew 19:9)

It must be noted that the above two verses are addressed to men, who had all the rights regarding family arrangements. These verses were recited to prevent men from divorcing their wives and thus subjecting them to poverty and loss of social status, as women in Jesus' day derived these through men. In that era, Jewish women could not initiate divorce.

> To the married I give this command—not I but the Lord—that the wife should not separate from her husband (but if she does separate, let her remain unmarried or else be reconciled to her husband), and that the husband should not divorce his wife. To the rest I say—I, and not the Lord—that if any believer has a wife who is an unbeliever, and she consents to live with him, he should not divorce her. And if any woman has a husband who is an unbeliever, and he consents to live with her, she should not divorce him. For the unbelieving husband is made holy through his wife, and the unbelieving wife is made holy through her husband. Otherwise, your children would be unclean, but as it is, they are holy. But if the unbelieving partner separates, let it be so; in such a case the brother or sister is not bound. It is to peace that God has called you. Wife, for all you know, you might save your husband. Husband, for all you know, you might save your wife. (I Cor. 7:10-16)

In cases of domestic violence, it is vital that all Christians understand that the once sacred covenant of marriage is broken not by the victimized wife but by the abusive husband. Whether he has committed adultery or not, the husband, by his abuse, has already been "unfaithful" to the covenant he made with his wife before God: promising to always be a loving and respectful intimate partner. Acts of domestic violence destroy this promise; they demonstrate neither love nor respect. What shatters a marriage and family is the criminal and sinful behavior perpetrated by an abusive husband, not the efforts of a violated wife to separate herself and her children from more harm. In addition, it must be said that regardless of whether a battering husband remains in the home, he has already "deserted" his wife (and children) by his inappropriate emotional, physical, psychological, sexual, and spiritual actions.

One other point must be made here. Wherever I travel, survivors tell stories about how Christian clergy and congregants pressure them into remaining in their abusive marriages because "God hates divorce." The saying comes from the book of Malachi. A prophet who lived during the second half of the fifth century B.C.E., Malachi's chief concern was that the Israelites' relationship to God was not as it should be. They had married foreign women, failed to give God what they should have, and even left God. They had forgotten God and treated God with dishonor. They failed to do what God required of them.[12] Although Malachi's saying about divorce is about God's marriage to Israel, many Christians have recited Malachi 2:16 as though it referred to relationships between human beings! And, like most biblical passages used against women, it is used with a significant portion left out. Catherine Clark Kroeger and Nancy Nason-Clark, in *No Place for Abuse,* explain:

> When we announce that [God] hates divorce, we do not add that the same verse declares that God hates violence. Indeed the Malachi 2:16 passage is translated alternatively by the New International Version thus: *"I hate divorce,"* says the Lord God of Israel, *"and I hate a man's covering his wife with violence as with his garment,"* says [God]. So guard yourself in your spirit, and do not break faith (emphasis added).[13]

Christians must be careful not to compromise battered women's support and safety. Espousing beliefs, teachings, traditions, or

Scripture out of its proper context to support our position against divorce, will not offer survivors sanctuary. Instead, this could cause women to experience more pain and maybe death. "I tried to talk with other Christians about my husband's abuse," asserts Janine Limas, now a domestic violence spokesperson with Interval House, who was married six years to a physically, psychologically, and spiritually abusive man. The responses she received from other churchgoers, she says, were not helpful. "They all replied, 'You just need to hang in there, you need to keep praying about your situation, you need to get your husband to come [to church], and you guys need to get some marriage counseling.' Then they told me, 'No matter what your husband does, remember that divorce is wrong.' This was the terrible advice I got from other Christians!"

We must remember that in cases of domestic violence, the marriage covenant is not broken by wives seeking safety (even if through separation or divorce), but by their husbands' violence.

Husbands' "God-given" Authority over Their Wives

It's the perfect setup to keep millions of Christian women entrapped in unhealthy and potentially lethal marriages: promoting the doctrine that God gives husbands authority and "headship" over their wives. Personally, I find the concept inconceivable. Why would a God of compassion, love, and mercy, a God embodied in Jesus' actions of mutuality and justice, a God who, through God's servant, Paul, declares "for all of you are one in Christ Jesus," a God of sensitivity, order women and men in a hierarchy? It doesn't add up. I believe that male headship is, in the literal sense, a man-made concept designed to maintain a patriarchal social system.

The verses from the Christian Scriptures most frequently cited to justify men's authority over women are Ephesians 5:21-33. Although Paul's guidelines here are for both husbands and wives worshiping in Christian churches near the city of Ephesus, over the centuries these passages have been used to elevate the status of men and put women down. Seldom do clergy members or congregants discuss the fact that nine of the twelve verses carry instructions for Christian husbands to follow. An inordinate amount of attention has been paid to what these verses tell wives, rather than what they demand of men. The passages clearly instruct husbands to love their wives as they do their own bodies. Nevertheless, the verses are often used to instruct women on what they are to do for their husbands—even those husbands who abuse their wives.

"Theologically, I knew my actions were wrong," admits Rev. Mark-Peter Lundquist, an ordained Christian minister and former batterer. Lundquist abused his wife, psychologically and spiritually, for a number of years. One way he did this, the spiritual leader now admits, was to manipulate Scripture. "I knew Ephesians 5:21 and beyond," Lundquist explains. "I was taught and I affirmed that these biblical verses are used by men to justify their abuse and control of women. It was a funny kind of schizophrenia: I knew how some men used these verses to justify their abusive actions, and to keep women in 'their place.' And I never wanted to be identified with these men. And yet, I was guilty of it myself. So there was a disconnection between my thinking and my behavior."

Even abuse survivors have been convinced by their perpetrators, pastors, and other Christians into believing that God views women as inferior to men. "My ex-husband would refer to the passages in Ephesians about the relationship between husbands and wives and tell me that man had 'responsibility' for woman," says Kim Smith King. "We both believed that God had, in the language I would have used at the time, 'lordship' over my life. Then my husband was next in terms of having 'lordship' over my life. So I was accountable and responsible to God and my husband, and I took direction from them both—even though my husband was abusing me. This was our church's teaching."

Let us take a closer look at what "headship" meant in early Christian thought. The Greek word *kephale,* often translated as "head," has a number of metaphorical uses in the Christian

Scriptures. Ordinarily it denotes "source," "origin," or "preeminence," rather than "authority over" or "ruler."[14] In an article addressing the classical concept of "head" as "source," Greek language scholar Catherine Clark Kroeger states:

> To declare that man was the source of woman, that she was bone of his bone and flesh of his flesh, was to give woman a nature like man's own. She was no longer of the substance of the animals but of man. She was a fit partner, his glory and his image. "Neither is the woman independent of the man nor the man of the woman in the Lord; for just as the woman is from the man, so man is from the woman, and all things are of God" (I Cor. 11:11,12).[15]

In the first century, the general Jewish and Greco-Roman understanding of marriage was that wives were to submit to their husbands in all things. Ephesians 5:24 reads, "Just as the church is subject to Christ, so also wives ought to be, in everything, to their husbands." But, as New Testament professor David Scholer points out, "[This] cultural understanding of marriage is significantly qualified for those in Christ, so that the passage teaches an overarching concept of mutual submission. In this context, *kephale* hardly means 'authority over,' especially in the leadership and authority-bearing sense for husbands over wives . . ."[16] What is clear, whether we are discussing first century or twenty-first century Christianity, is this: there is no justification for Christian husbands to abuse their wives in any way, at any time.

> Although the notion of husband as the head is often quoted nowadays as a justification for domestic violence, this is not the thrust of the New Testament passages. The headship image was to make both husband and wife part of the same body, dependent for their very existence upon one another. The husband was to view her not as attached to another family, but tenderly, as part of his own body, "bone of his bone and flesh of his flesh."[17]

Let us now turn our attention to another often quoted biblical concept: female submission. This idea has also been frequently misrepresented by abusers, clergy members, and churchgoers to excuse men's violence and to blame women for their own victimization.

Wives' "God-ordained" Duty to Submit to Their Husbands

Many of us who grew up in the Christian church were trained to think that Paul's famous instructions to husbands and wives in the book of Ephesians, chapter 5, begins and ends with verse 22: "Wives, submit to your husbands as to the Lord" (NIV). Proclaimed by clergy and other pastoral ministers from pulpits and at weddings, and by parents, teachers, and other congregants as well, Ephesians 5:22 has established a foundation on which countless numbers of Christian marriages have been built.

The verse has also been a perfect setup for millions of women to suffer acts of domestic violence.

"I had been molested by my brother when I was very young and again as a teenager," says Lani, a Christian woman who married her Christian husband, Mark, when she was seventeen. "Before we got married, I told my husband all about the abuse because I thought it might pose a problem," Lani explains. "But he never really acknowledged my past and never thought it would be an issue." Despite her husband's rather naive attitude, Lani says the sexual abuse she suffered from her brother caused major problems when she and Mark sought to be sexually intimate. "We had a lot of difficulties because of the abuse I suffered in the past. I would often cry and not want to become sexually involved. It was a very emotionally traumatic time for me."

It was during these times, Lani recalls, that her husband began reminding her of the "duties" she had to perform as a Christian wife. "In all other things—Bible study, prayer, a husband's responsibility to treat his wife with love and respect—Mark never took the lead," Lani says. "But he was sure quick to point out what I, as a

Christian wife, needed to do for him sexually. In spite of his full awareness of the abuse I went through from my brother, Mark kept telling me that it was my duty to 'render my due,' in other words, to have sex whenever he desired simply because he was my husband. Mark also recited a lot of the teachings from the apostle Paul, which I still think are wonderful writings. But my husband used the teachings about wifely submission to control me, to get what he wanted when he wanted it."

Lani's story is not unique. Across the globe, countless Christian women are being abused in all kinds of ways by their Christian husbands. In many of these situations, the male batterers cite Ephesians 5:22 to justify their criminal and sinful behavior. As might be expected, these perpetrators intentionally neglect to consider the full content of the aforementioned nine verses (Ephesians 5:21-33, quoted on page 59), which instruct Christian husbands on how to treat their wives with love and respect. Sad to say, Christian clergy and laity are often equally neglectful. Why?

Paul's admonition in the book of Ephesians to Christian husbands and wives begins not at verse 22, but at verse 21: "Submit to one another out of reverence for Christ." Inclusion of this one sentence puts on a whole new light and brings clarity to the entire passage. No longer can Christians view marriage as a male hierarchical union. Instead, we are challenged to observe the covenant of matrimony like God and Christ intended: as a mutual and egalitarian bond.

The Greek word *hupotasso,* which is commonly translated as "to submit," has several different meanings. In fact, there are a cluster of words commonly understood to be related to "submission" in the Christian Scriptures: *hupotasso* (a verb meaning to submit, but also to behave responsibly toward another, to align oneself with, or to relate to another in a meaningful way); *hupotaktes* (an adjective meaning submissive, but more commonly, behaving in an orderly or proper fashion); *anupotaktos* (an adjective that is opposite to *hupotaktes:* disorderly, irresponsible, confused, or lacking meaning); and *hupotage* (a noun meaning submission, attachment, or copy).[18]

In essence, Paul is instructing Christian husbands and wives to behave responsibly toward one another, align themselves and to relate to one another in a meaningful and respectful way. Thus, in Christian marriages, there must never be a hierarchical structure. Even when husbands are both loving and respectful, when there is no abuse whatsoever in the nuptial, male headship and female submission work against wives because this type of union disallows a woman to be a full and equal partner with her husband. The hierarchical structure is ultimately disadvantageous for husbands as well because it prevents them from reaping the benefits of sharing life with a woman who is equal to him in every way.

Most important, equality and mutuality in marriage, rather than female submission and male headship, help both women and men to live out the covenant God and Christ intended for Christians. There is no biblical justification for acts of domestic violence. Husbands have no right—not by God, Jesus, Scripture, beliefs, teachings, or tradition—to abuse their wives in any way. Equality and mutuality in marriage also help Christian women to understand it is never their duty, responsibility, or lot in life to have to endure the illegal and sinful actions of their Christian husbands, whether these inappropriate actions are emotional, physical, psychological, sexual, or spiritual in nature. Domestic violence is *always* worthy of condemnation.

The Sacred Virtue of Forgiveness

I am constantly reminded by many Christians, both clergy and lay, about the sacredness of forgiveness. Wherever I conduct domestic violence awareness trainings—in rural, urban, or suburban communities, and among people from various denominational, cultural, and racial backgrounds—forgiveness is held in the same high regard as faith, hope, and love.

Unfortunately, there has been a misunderstanding of what forgiveness actually entails. A result of this misunderstanding is that individuals who have been wronged end up being pressured or rushed into saying they forgive their transgressor(s). Specifically, survivors of domestic violence are told it is their duty to forgive and forget the damage caused by their abusive and violent partners, that forgiveness will solve the problem. They are further instructed that forgiveness is the same as reconciliation. These claims are simply not true. They are nevertheless asserted by perpetrators (as a way to maintain power and control over the people they violate), clergy, other pastoral ministers, and laity. And, just as with the other issues discussed in this chapter, God, Jesus, and Scripture are often invoked by those who tell battered women they must quickly forgive their abusers.

"At one point he became very angry with me and, somehow, got me in the position where I was flat on my back and he had a wire coat hanger to my neck," recalls Kim Smith King, who suffered nine years under the abuse perpetrated by her Christian husband. "I found myself constantly watching and waiting for signs that would indicate what he was going to do next. At the same time, I knew his violent behavior would come out of nowhere. So the sense was of me always holding my breath, of keeping all my senses open, like radar. I tried to create situations or create a climate in which there wasn't a great deal of tension: keeping the children good, turning in the receipts he expected from me, not talking back much. This approach worked for a while, perhaps a day or even for a week. But then there would be some incident—or no incident—and he would resume more overt, abusive behavior."

Despite her husband's illegal and immoral actions, Kim was told by her perpetrator, by one of her pastors, and by several members of the church she was attending that she must forgive him. "My husband would turn everything on me. He'd say, 'You call yourself a Christian, yet you're unwilling to forgive me.' He'd also say the same thing whenever he perceived that I didn't forgive his abuse quickly enough. In his way of thinking, I was the un-Christian person with the problem. And my church taught me that forgiveness meant to 'turn the other cheek' and to forgive 'seven times seventy.' In other words, according to them, I needed to always forgive my husband for everything."

Lani, a healthcare provider, received a similar message from both her Christian husband, Mark, who abused her all nine years of their marriage, and from members of the church where the couple worshiped. "My husband constantly called me inappropriate names: 'dumb,' 'stupid,' and 'slut,'" Lani says. "When we'd have members of the congregation over to our home for dinner, he'd often say and do cruel things to me. For example, one day I tried to bring lunch to Mark at his job site. But, having a terrible sense of direction, I got lost and never located him. That evening Mark read me the riot act, calling me all sorts of terrible names in front of his family and our neighbors, all of them people from our church. At some point he threw a whole bunch of stuff in my arms and yelled, 'Now, woman, go to the kitchen and cook dinner!' He thought this was funny but I felt totally humiliated."

Seeking distance from her husband after suffering for years under his emotional and psychological battering, Lani made plans to divorce Mark. But she found herself rebuked by both her family and members of her church. They all told Lani she needed to forgive her husband and then everything would be okay. "There was a major double standard going on in my church," Lani says. "Mark would call me all these terrible names—and many people from our church witnessed this inappropriate behavior firsthand—but no one ever turned their back on him. Although my husband never hit me, his verbal and emotional abuse was certainly contrary to the teachings of the Bible. But the congregation did nothing to address Mark's behavior. Instead, the church kept reminding me about the sinful nature of divorce and the importance of my being a forgiving Christian wife."

Lani eventually divorced Mark and was shunned by her family and congregation. Still, the survivor says she made the right choice to get out of her abusive marriage. She offers words of encouragement to other victimized Christian women struggling with the issue of forgiveness. "I now know that a man is not entitled to abuse any woman; that's not at all what the Bible teaches," Lani says. "I've now forgiven my former husband, but on my own terms. And I don't believe forgiveness is demanded of an abuse victim, not like my former husband and members of my former congregation taught. Forgiveness doesn't mean you have to say abuse is okay—because it never is. I want all battered women to realize that God does not want any of his children to suffer—not in any way."

In order to better serve domestic violence survivors like Kim and Lani, Christians must first have a clear understanding of what forgiveness is and what it is not. Forgiveness is the decision on the part of a person who has been abused, betrayed, or wronged to let go of, or put aside, the justifiable anger, bitterness, and hurt that arises from being victimized.[19] Although forgiveness can be achieved in a short period of time, it is often a very long-term process. This is especially true when a victimized person has been wronged repeatedly and over a significant period of time, as is usually the case in situations of domestic violence. Thus, suggesting or pressuring an abuse victim into forgiving her transgressor will accomplish nothing positive. On the contrary, this type of approach runs the risk of causing battered women more agony. In addition, so-called "biblical truths"—which are usually offered out of context—prove to be more harmful than helpful to survivors struggling with the complicated issue of forgiveness. Therefore, here are some statements Christians should not use when talking to battered women about abuse:

- Jesus tells us in the Gospel of Matthew, "If someone strikes you on the right cheek, turn to him the other also."
- Forgive and forget.
- Remember that the Bible says, "If you forgive people when they sin against you, God will also forgive you. But if you do not forgive people their sins, God will not forgive your sins."
- Jesus says we are to forgive others "seventy times seven."
- If you don't forgive your husband, then it's an indication that you're not practicing Christian love.
- The Bible says, "All have sinned and fallen short of the glory of

God." Your husband sinned, but so have you. You must forgive him.

- Jesus warns, "Do not judge, or you too will be judged."
- Only those without sin, says God, should cast stones at others.
- To err is human; to forgive, divine. (This is from the writings of Alexander Pope, not the Bible, but Christians commonly quote it in the context of abusive situations.)[20]

As mentioned earlier, forgiveness is often mistakenly equated by Christians (and others) with forgetting, with the notion that forgiving will make everything okay, and with reconciliation. Let us discuss each of these ideas.

Forgive and Forget

It is unrealistic to think a survivor will forget the punishment she has suffered from her husband or boyfriend. Recall for a moment any devastating occurrence in your own life. Even if this event happened once, and long ago, it is still remembered. So why would a battered woman forget ongoing acts of emotional, physical, psychological, sexual, and spiritual treachery? Listen to the voice of Leslie as she describes her continued agony over the abuse she suffered forty years ago from her husband, Ted: "As far as my Christianity, I have a deeper relationship with God and a deeper knowledge of his love for me," the survivor says. "But I still go through times of self-doubt about God's love toward me. I think it'll take a lifetime to get over all I've suffered, and to get over the feelings that God is punishing me for something I've done. I'll probably go to my grave not totally believing God loves me."

Many survivors have told me they have felt pressured by their pastors and by other Christians to "forgive and forget" just as "God and Jesus instruct in the Bible." But, the oft-quoted phrase is not to be found anywhere in either the Hebrew Bible or Christian Scriptures. It is a saying from William Shakespeare's *The Tragedy of King Lear,* spoken by Lear to his daughter Cordelia, whom he has wronged: "You must bear with me. Pray you now, forget, and forgive. I am old and foolish."[21]

Forgiveness Will Make Everything Okay

The problem with the belief that forgiveness will make everything okay, especially when this phrase is applied to victims of domestic violence, is that the equation presupposes that a survivor's actions can change an abuser's behavior. This is simply not true. As discussed in the previous chapter, batterers—and batterers alone—are responsible for the abuse and violence they perpetrate. It is up to them to repent, to seek help from a batterers' intervention program, and to take the necessary long-term spiritual and psychological steps to change their sinful behavior. Unfortunately, most batterers are much more concerned with getting what they want when they want it than in doing the necessary hard work to effect healthy and lasting changes in their lives. Therefore, we must never tell a survivor that forgiving her abuser will make everything okay in her marriage or intimate partnership. Espousing such a belief could cause a victim to suffer greater harm or even death.

Forgiveness as Reconciliation

As stated previously, forgiveness is the process of letting go, or putting aside our right to be angry, bitter, and so forth, for having been hurt by another human being. We can choose to forgive someone without forgetting how we were wronged by that person, we can choose to forgive someone without saying what they did to us is excusable, and we can choose to forgive someone without restoring a relationship with them. Reconciliation, on the other hand, begins with the notion of restoration. It is the decision on the part of two or more people to reclaim, through mutually trustworthy behavior, a relationship that has been broken by abuse, betrayal, and other wrongs. It is precisely here that equating forgiveness with reconciliation, especially in cases of domestic violence, can be very risky. Although a battered woman may choose to let go of her justifiable anger, bitterness, hurt, and so forth, for being beaten, cursed, harassed, raped, and/or betrayed in other ways by a man who promised to always be faithful, loving, and respectful, the survivor may not choose to "restore" a relationship with this man because he cannot be trusted.

Clergy, other pastoral ministers, and laity must always keep in the front of their minds a solemn truth: perpetrators of domestic violence rarely take responsibility for the damage they cause their wives, girlfriends, or children. Unless a batterer is willing to work long and hard at becoming a nonabusive and nonviolent member of society (remember, a claim of quick spiritual transformation "by God" is simply another tactic used to control a victim—and us), then suggesting to a survivor that she restore her relationship with this man is inappropriate. Even if an offender demonstrates healthy lifestyle changes over a long period of time, the victimized woman still has the right not to restore the partnership. Therefore, Christians must never pressure a survivor into reconciling a relationship torn apart by acts of domestic violence.

How Christians Can Help

Here are some specific ways Christian clergy and congregation members can help a victimized woman who is struggling with the complicated issue of forgiveness:

Be long on listening and short on advice. By listening more and talking less, ordained ministers and Christian laity provide a survivor with a supportive spiritual presence and minimize the temptation to blurt out the well-meant but trite statements discussed earlier in the chapter. In addition, silence gives a survivor the freedom, space, and time to work on the often long and difficult process of forgiveness.

Stand with a survivor in her pursuit of justice. Our own feelings of fear and helplessness, along with other factors, make it much easier for most members of the church and society to excuse and/or justify the abusive behavior of a male perpetrator than to stand with a female victim on the side of justice. Although it can be costly, the appropriate position for the church to take is to support the victim and the many difficult decisions she must make. This includes offering our support even if the survivor decides to permanently leave her abusive partner or file criminal charges against him. If a trial does pursue, having three or four members from the congregation in the courtroom during the proceedings communicates a clear and important message: the number-one concern of the church is the safety and well being of the survivor and her children.

Don't pressure a victim into forgiving. A survivor must be given time to work on the process of forgiveness without any pressure from others. This may include supporting a survivor's decision to not forgive for the time being.[22] "Waiting patiently with the victim until she is ready to forgive may be the most charitable and compassionate act the church can offer," writes Marie M. Fortune. "In these ways, we take seriously the power of forgiveness to bring people to healing."[23]

Conclusion

Would God and Jesus Christ condone acts of domestic violence? I think all of us would agree that the answer to this question is a resounding *no*. This being the case, then why do so many Christian leaders and laity excuse or overlook the emotional, physical, psychological, sexual, and spiritual atrocities perpetrated by men who claim to be Christian upon women? And why would we put our faith in beliefs, teachings, and traditions that clearly make it easier for men to terrorize women and then use these doctrine as divine justification?

Marriage is a sacred bond, but only when both husbands and wives commit to the biblical virtues of love and respect will such a union be sustained and grow. Divorce is a devastating event but, in cases of domestic violence, we must always remember that the bond of the marriage covenant was broken not by the victimized wife, but by the perpetrating husband. In essence, he was both "unfaithful" to and "deserting" of his female intimate partner by his criminal and sinful behavior. Embracing the doctrine of male headship and female submission is wrong. These teachings set up an imbalance of power in a marriage or other intimate partnership, making it much easier for men to abuse women and to then claim divine privilege. Finally, while forgiveness is a sacred virtue, battered women must never be forced or coerced into forgiving. Forgiveness must never be used interchangeably with forgetting, with acceptance of abuse, or with the concept of reconciliation.

Let us work together to prevent and to eliminate acts of domestic violence in our world. Let us also speak against all doctrine that encourages, excuses, or justifies the abuse men perpetrate against their wives, female intimate partners, and against all other women.

Questions for Discussion

1. Which is more sacred: the safety of women or the sanctity of the marriage covenant? Discuss the risk factors associated with telling an abused woman that her marriage must be "saved at all costs."

2. According to the Christian Scriptures, are there any circumstances when divorce is permissible? Name and discuss them. In cases of domestic violence, what role do perpetrators take in breaking the covenant of marriage?

3. Discuss at least five possible negative outcomes resulting from the male headship/female submission model in a marriage or intimate partnership.

4. How do you define forgiveness? Name and discuss at least five potential ways the three concepts equated with forgiveness in this chapter can be harmful to survivors of domestic violence.

5. How will you now work together as a congregation to ensure that God, Jesus Christ, Scripture, and doctrine are not used against victims of domestic violence?

3.

Teen Dating and
Relationship Violence:
In and Out of the Church

Like adult intimate partner abuse, incidents of teen dating and teen relationship violence occur at a phenomenal rate worldwide. In America alone, it is estimated that one in three girls will experience abuse in a dating relationship by the time she graduates from high school. Many experts in the field believe this number is unrealistically low. Dr. Jill Murray, an author and psychotherapist, speaks to thousands of students and parents in high schools around the country each year on abusive teen relationships. She calls the one-in-three statistic "a gross underestimation."[1] Even by this conservative figure, the therapist points out in her book *But I Love Him,* "more than eight million girls per year in the United States alone suffer at the hands of a violent boyfriend before their eighteenth birthday."[2] (Teen boys are also victimized, and their stories need to be heard as well. However, in this book due to the fact that girls and women are more adversely affected by intimate partner violence than are boys and men in regard to injury rates, injury severity, etc., we will focus on female victims and male perpetrators.)

Christian girls are no less vulnerable to attack than are girls from the general public. Although many church leaders and lay people choose, out of denial, fear, and helplessness, to minimize or totally overlook the problem within their own congregation and community, episodes of teen dating and teen relationship violence do occur in relationships between young people who attend Christian churches every week. "My first boyfriend raped me when I was twelve," says Christie Corpuz, a longtime Christian, age twenty-six at the time I interviewed her. For years she suffered emotional, physical, psychological, sexual, and spiritual abuse, first from her father and then from a series of boyfriends during her teen years. All of the perpetrators, including Christie's father, claimed to be Christians, even as they were carrying out their acts of terrorism upon her. The survivor still vividly recalls how she was objectified by her first boyfriend, whom she dated until she was fifteen.

"I was just his plaything," Christie says. "The most degrading thing he would do was rape me at church, when everybody else was in the sanctuary and we'd be in children's church. And he'd do the same at church camp." Although many of the adult Christians knew that she was being abused, Christie says, they did nothing to try to help her. "I had all these bruises on me that were visible to everyone, but no one ever asked me about them. My boyfriend's mother and brothers also knew what he was doing. But they kept begging me not to tell on him. 'Please don't say anything to anyone else,' they pleaded. 'We don't want him to get into any trouble.'" At age fifteen, Christie and her mother decided to tell the associate pastor at their church all about the three years of abuse Christie suffered from this Christian young man. But the spiritual leader blamed Christie for her own victimization. "When Mom and I told the pastor about all the rapes and all the beatings I received from my boyfriend, the first thing the minister asked was, 'What did you do to entice him?' We knew then that this pastor would be of no help whatsoever."

What constitutes teen dating and relationship violence? Are there warning signs for parents, professionals, and other concerned citizens to watch for that may indicate a girl is being violated? How can Christian parents talk to their daughters and sons about this problem? What can the church do to help prevent and eliminate teen dating and relationship violence?

Before we delve into these questions, let us consider the story of a young Christian woman named Tina Croucher. Born into a loving family and raised in the church, Tina was, according to her mother, Elsa, "a very spoiled child, doted upon, loved, and, like her father, strong willed and knew exactly what she wanted." At age sixteen, Tina brought home her first boyfriend for her parents to meet.

Tina's Story

God,

I don't really know where to begin. You know everything that happened with [my boyfriend and me] this time last year, but I'm with him again. I truly believe and see that he has changed, but he still has a bad attitude. Most of the time he treats me good, and I'm happy. But when we argue and fight, sometimes I wonder why I let myself get into this mess again. My relationship with my parents is going down real fast, but it's just because the things that I want to be able to talk to them about they won't listen to. So, therefore, what are we supposed to talk about? I feel really far away from them. When I got into my wreck [which totaled my car in October 1992], I knew you were right beside me holding my hand. I could just feel it. Now I really feel like you're talking to me and telling me to straighten my act up. God, you know how hard it is to change something. I want to become closer to you, but I need help. Please help me to take the time to sit down and read my Bible and to talk to you for a few minutes a day. I'm really sorry for how I've acted to you. You saved me in my wreck. God, I love you, and thank you so much. I realize that the only thing you want in return is for me to love you and serve you. That shouldn't be too much for anybody to handle so, as of now, I would like to rededicate my life to you. I want to serve you and to be happy for eternity. Thank you, God, for making me the strong, beautiful person that I am today, and the even stronger more beautiful Christian that I am now, tomorrow, and for eternity. Please help me to reach out to others, and to help the people that need help. Thank you for giving me so many chances. Now I know that if there should be a next time, I would be ready. I love you, Lord! Talk to you tomorrow.

Love, Tina

("Letter to God," December 7, 1992)

"He was a big and handsome young man who played high school football," says Jim Croucher as he reflects upon his daughter's first boyfriend. "At first he appeared to be a nice young man, but we were told that he had a very violent temper. He threatened teachers all the way from grade school up into high school. He was suspended several times because of fights. He was even kicked off the football team for being too violent. Even around us he began to show character flaws. He'd lose his temper while playing basketball or fly off the handle for one reason or another."

At first, Tina Croucher defended her boyfriend, telling her parents that they must be "imagining" his violence. But Elsa Croucher insists that she and her husband were not imagining the marks that began appearing on their daughter's body. "We didn't know what teen dating violence was then," Tina's mother admits. "But we started questioning Tina about bruises on her face, arms, and legs. Tina would tell us that she and her boyfriend had just been playing touch football or basketball; she always had an excuse."

Jim and Elsa accepted their daughter's explanation. "Tina had always been a very open and honest young lady," Elsa says. "She always talked things over with me. Sometimes, she would even tell me things that I would rather she not tell me. Consequently, it never once occurred to me that Tina was lying to us about the bruises." But one day a friend of Elsa's, who worked at Tina and her boyfriend's school, told Elsa they needed to talk. "We have two high schools in our district," Elsa says. "And Tina's boyfriend had transferred to our daughter's school so that he could keep watch over her at all times. Well, my friend called me and said she had witnessed the young man 'slapping Tina around.' A teacher at the school confirmed that my daughter had simply been talking to another male, and her boyfriend came down the hall, grabbed Tina, and slammed her into a locker. The boy was suspended from school, and my husband and I told our daughter, 'You cannot continue to see this young man. This is inappropriate behavior, we do not agree with this, and this cannot go on.'"

Tina followed the wishes of her parents. And, according to Elsa, that's when their daughter's boyfriend began manifesting overt violent behavior. "He would call our house and leave horrible phone messages," Elsa says. "He stalked Tina. In fact, she was so scared at one point that she and I slept in a different part of the house because she kept saying her boyfriend knew exactly where the bed was in her room. But we hesitated to file any charges against this young man; we just kept hoping and praying it would soon be over, that he would go away. We told ourselves that the young man would soon calm down, get over Tina, and go on with his life."

The inappropriate behavior continued, however, and Jim and Elsa eventually filed charges against the young man. He spent a night in jail. But when they asked Tina to never speak with her boyfriend again, she became upset with her parents. "She thought we were being terribly un-Christian in our attitude," Elsa says. "However, we realized this young man was such a charmer that if he came around Tina with his sweet smile and all of his charming words she would believe in him again. And that's exactly what happened. By this time, our daughter had turned eighteen. So we told her, 'We can no longer choose your friends for you, but this man is not allowed on our property, and he is not allowed to call our house.'"

Telling Tina one day how much he had changed, the young man boasted he was now a wonderful person. "My daughter believed every charming word that came out of this man's mouth," Elsa says. "She believed everything was going to be wonderful. So she decided to date him again."

Four days before Christmas in 1992, eighteen-year-old Tina, who was now a freshman at Miami University in Ohio and held a part-time job, had a day off. Her parents, with whom she was living, went to work as usual in the morning, and Tina decided to sleep in. As she lay in her bed, she received an unscheduled visit from the man she had dated on and off the past eighteen months. This young man, who had only recently boasted about all the positive changes he had made in his life, the man who charmed Tina time and again with his sweet smile and glowing promises, entered her bedroom quietly, so as not to disturb her. And he demonstrated just how much he had changed: He murdered Tina with a gunshot to her head while she lay sleeping. An hour later, the young man killed himself.

"I pray to God that no other parent ever has to go through the tragedy Elsa and I faced," Jim says softly. He offered a warning to all parents with teenage daughters: "Parents must make themselves knowledgeable about teen dating violence. They have to know what to look for and what to do if their daughters experience this situation."

Behaviors That Constitute Teen Dating and Teen Relationship Violence

The tactics that abusive teen boys use against their girlfriends are similar to those employed by men against their wives and other intimate female partners. These include verbal and emotional abuse, sexual abuse, and physical abuse. (A special warning to

Christians: a teenage boy will misuse the Bible to claim male superiority over his teenage female partners, just as a man uses Scripture to justify the authority he takes over his wife and/or girlfriend. The boy learns this from his father, pastors, teachers, and sometimes from his mother—who is trying to make him a "good Christian young man.") Abuse is a tool that helps boys get what they want, when they want it, and to maintain power and control over their female victims.

"I was very sexist, very chauvinistic," confesses David Garcia. In his teen years, David used various abuse tactics to control girls. The twenty-two-year-old former batterer is now a domestic violence educator in the domestic violence program that saved his family's life—California's Interval House. David is also a leader in Interval House's Second Generation, an acting troupe that specializes in working against abusive teen relationship and domestic violence. (We'll learn more about the Second Generation in chapter 4.)

"I was really controlling," David says. "I remember one particular girl I dated. If she talked with any other guy, I would do things to find out what she was talking about. And I got other people to spy on her. I'd also get really angry with her in front of other people, and it didn't matter who was around." David says that at the time he was not aware of the reasons why he engaged in abusive behavior. "I just knew the tactics worked. I knew my actions were effective at getting what I wanted, when I wanted it. All my other male friends kept telling me 'you've gotta keep your bitch in check.' In the crowd I hung around, a boy was actually looked down upon if he didn't act that way toward a girl."

Let us turn our attention to specific abuse tactics used to control and hurt teenage girls in dating relationships.

Verbal and Emotional Abuse

Christie Corpuz describes the devastating and lingering effect of the verbal and emotional abuse she suffered as a teenage girl. "The boy I dated from age twelve to fifteen was, like me, raised in the church," the survivor states. "He even claimed to be a Christian. And yet, this same boy constantly called me a 'slut,' 'whore,' 'bitch,' and 'cunt.' He especially liked calling me a 'cunt' because he knew I found this word so offensive. He also isolated me: calling my friends to check on me, for example. One time he found out I went to a school dance and had danced with another boy. My boyfriend beat the crap out of me for doing that. His physical abuse was awful, but the verbal and emotional abuse was even more degrading. And I still carry emotional scars from that relationship to this day."

Dr. Jill Murray comments in her book *But I Love Him:*

> Verbal and emotional abuse can be the most devastating type of power and control. In this setup, the boy systemically degrades your daughter's feeling of self-worth by calling her names, blaming her for his own faults, making accusations, humiliating her in public, destroying objects that are special to her, telling her she's crazy, and using menacing looks and intimidation. Think about this for a moment: a broken bone can heal and bruises fade, but without positive self-esteem, your daughter is an invalid. When a person, especially one we value highly, degrades our very soul, how long do you think it takes to heal? Sometimes we never do.[3]

Rodney Kahao knows all about emotional and verbal abuse tactics. He runs batterers' groups for the PACT (Parents And Children Together) Family Peace Center in Honolulu and is a volunteer with the Salvation Army's Substance Abuse Program. A self-described born-again Christian since 1985, Kahao is candid about the abusive tactics he used in his teen relationships with girls. "When I was thirteen, I began dating a girl a few years older than I was. I started to control her immediately. You know, I'd tell her who she could and couldn't see, how she could and couldn't dress, where she could and couldn't go, and what she could and couldn't do. And I started controlling her verbally as well, calling her 'bitch,' 'whore,' 'slut,' 'stupid,' and many other nasty names. When these tactics didn't work, I began to beat her." Although he expressed remorse following an episode of emotional, physical, and verbal battering, Kahao now admits he always blamed all the young women he dated for the abuse he perpetrated. "I was always really sorry after I hurt any of my girlfriends," he says. "But I made it clear to all of them that my behavior was their fault. 'If you wouldn't have done what you did or said what you said,' I'd insist, 'then I wouldn't have had to treat you the way I did.' I now see I took no responsibility for the emotional, verbal, and physical abuse I used against so many girls."

Let's look closely at other verbal and emotional abuse tactics.

Cell Phones and Pagers. In our technologically advanced world, cell phones and pagers are used by some teenage boys to maintain power and control over their female victims. "Incessant phone calls and pages are basically stalking behaviors," says Jerry Coffee, Employee Assistance Counselor with the Straub Employee Assistance Program in Honolulu. For a number of years, Coffee has worked with children and teens who witness and experience first-hand various forms of abuse. "Anything that causes teens in their gut to think or feel it might not be right, then it's probably not right. Incessant phone calls and pages might not, in and of them-selves, be abusive. But, in terms of a healthy balance for teenagers, these actions exhibit an attempt by one teen to control the freedom of another teen."

Dr. Jill Murray concurs:

> Boys frequently give their girlfriends a pager and/or cell phone so that they can remain in constant contact. This enables the boy to check up on the girl as often as he likes. Usually this means that when he pages her, she must call him back within a specified period. Of course, it doesn't start that way; a boy will tell his girl-friend that he is giving her these gifts so that they can stay in touch and remain close. Sometimes they invent cute little secret codes that only the two of them know, such as, "When I page you and enter the number two, you'll know that I'm thinking of you and I love you!" What teenage girl wouldn't think that was special? Every time her pager goes off with a two on it, she feels like the luckiest girl in the world. Eventually, the boy becomes angry if anyone else pages her,

even her parents, because it intrudes on their time together. It also means that for that moment someone else has access to her attention. He wants to know exactly who paged her and why. Boys also think if they are paying for their girlfriend's cell phone, they have a right to know who's calling.[4]

"I Love You" and Other Sweet Nothings, Isolation, and Threats. Declarations of love can work to reinforce other abuse tactics. The teenage perpetrator will proclaim his undying love for his female victim, shower her with gifts and words of affection, begin to isolate her from friends and family, and then threaten her (and those individuals dear to her) if she decides to leave him. "The control started right away," recalls Brenda, a longtime Christian and a survivor of teen dating violence. "The first time I phoned my dad, my boyfriend, Martin, began to isolate me. He told me how my father and mother were trying to rule my life, and how my friends weren't looking out for my best interest either. Within a matter of three months, he asked me to marry him. Even though I didn't love Martin, I thought if somebody really cared for me that much then I wanted to be around him. In reality, it was Martin who wanted to control me. When I would wear certain clothes, he'd ask, 'Who are you trying to impress?' or, 'Is there somebody at work I need to know about?' Wherever I would go, he wanted to go with me. He even said, 'If you leave me I'll just die!' Or, he'd insinuate he couldn't be a good Christian without me, and it would all be my fault for breaking up with him. All this drama: the lies, manipulation, isolation, and other acts of control, were done by Martin to keep me in the relationship. And, for a long, long time, these tactics worked."

Lorena has her own story to tell. For several years she was abused, both verbally and emotionally, by the boy she was dating. He used inappropriate tactics such as those described by Brenda. And when Lorena attempted to leave this abusive young man, he threatened her life.

Lorena's Story

"It all started when I was in junior high, when I was in eighth grade," recalls Lorena, now age twenty-two. The survivor now works for Interval House Crisis Shelters, located in Los Angeles and Orange Counties, as a youth educator and domestic violence youth advocate. "I was fourteen, and my boyfriend was fifteen and in ninth grade. He went to the same junior high as I did, so a lot of my friends knew who he was. Actually, the whole school knew who he was because he was so popular. Everybody thought of him as this nice and gentle guy. The type of guy who would cross an ocean just to give you a flower. All the girls were crazy about him. He was the cutest guy on campus and caused all the girls to get the giggles each time he passed by them. So once he started to talk to me, and wanted to know my phone number, I felt really special. You know, the guy everyone else is after is after me. I just couldn't believe I ended up with the guy every other girl wanted. That was really cool!"

Lorena says she initially felt good about all the affection and constant attention. Her boyfriend would bring her roses, call her every night, and tell Lorena she was the love of his life, his soul mate, and that she was perfect. All of these statements were made shortly after the couple began dating. "I thought, 'Wow, I'm the center of attention in this guy's life!'" Lorena says. Having never been made to feel so special by a guy, she was overwhelmed. "I thought the world of him," she admits. "And I really did believe everything he was telling me at the time."

Lorena eventually began to feel uneasy. Her boyfriend became more and more upset if she wasn't home when he'd call. "He'd ask, 'How come you weren't home when I phoned you? You know I always call you at this time.' He'd make it seem like he had made such an effort. You know, that it took so much out of him that I wasn't home waiting by the phone at the time he called. So I began to feel like I had messed up because I wasn't there for him when he needed me most."

Lorena says that her boyfriend also wanted his name written on her hand in ink at all times. "At first, if I forgot to do this, he'd quickly take out a pen and write his name on me himself. However, a little further down the line, say, a month or two into the relationship, he asked 'Why don't we just engrave my name on your hand?' So he got a needle and, literally, scarred my hand with his name. He did this, my boyfriend proudly told me, so everyone would know that I was 'his.'"

As the relationship continued, Lorena began to notice that her boyfriend's "affection" tapered while his acts of control and isolation increased. "My boyfriend began to isolate me more and more. He wanted no one to talk to me and wanted me to talk to no one. I couldn't speak to anybody else, especially other boys. My boyfriend even began starting rumors about me. He told my friends I talked about them behind their backs. His lies were designed to further isolate me—to make all my friends angry so they would go away. He also began calling me all sorts of terrible names: 'bitch,' 'slut,' 'whore,' and would accuse me of sleeping with other guys, even though I wasn't even having sex with him. I felt totally isolated and totally controlled by this guy."

Lorena says she knew she had to get out of the relationship after a very terrifying incident at her boyfriend's house. "He had learned from the guys he always sent around to spy on me that I had a male friend," she explains. "There was nothing inappropriate about my relationship with this other guy; we were just good friends. Well, one day my boyfriend took me to his house and said he had a surprise for me. Taking me to his bedroom, he reached into one of the dresser drawers and pulled out a gun. He had this cute smile on his face and seemed really excited about the gun. He said, 'I don't like you talking to that other guy. Why would you even want to be friends with him?' He then reached into the drawer again and got three bullets. He placed one of the bullets in my hand and kept two in his hand."

Holding one of the bullets high in the air, Lorena's boyfriend spoke in a very calm, deliberate voice. "He said, 'This bullet is for your friend. If you don't stop talking to him, I'm going to kill him.' He then calmly put that bullet into the chamber of the gun. Next, he lifted the second bullet into the air and said, 'This is for my heart when you break it. If you ever break up with me it won't be your words that break my heart, but instead this bullet.'" Terrified, the teen girl listened to her boyfriend as he explained what would happen with the third bullet. "He took my hand, the one holding the bullet he had given me, and softly said 'If you don't stop seeing that other guy, or if you decide to ever leave me, this will be the bullet that will kill you.'"

Lorena did eventually get out of that relationship. But, as we will see later in this chapter, she continues to struggle, both spiritually and emotionally, as a result of the years of verbal and emotional abuse she suffered from her boyfriend.

Sexual Abuse

Leading a three-hour discussion at a Christian church on the behaviors that constitute abuse and violence in teen and adult intimate relationships, I was engrossed by the candid comments of a woman in her early seventies. For more than half a century, this woman had been married to an ordained deacon, and both husband and wife were highly respected church and community leaders. To a group consisting of fifty women and girls ranging in age from fifteen to eighty, she said, "My husband has never offered me even one iota of true passion in all these years. Our so-called lovemaking has always been abusive, consisting of him demanding sex, of him forcing me to engage in acts that I find pornographic, and has always consisted of my husband putting me down sexually by saying I am as warm as a 'meat locker,' 'frozen fish,' and that my private parts are like an 'ice box.'" Turning to the other workshop attendees, the woman asked a simple but very revealing question. "Have any of the rest of you ever experienced similar situations with your husbands or boyfriends?" Every person in the room, including the twenty or so teenage girls, raised their hands.

Sexual abuse in both teen and adult intimate relationships happens around the world. However, among teens it is especially pervasive because adolescents most often lack the experience and knowledge to discern appropriate sexual behavior. Furthermore, because teens are generally very reluctant to discuss their concerns (especially those about sexual matters) with adults, girls who decide to disclose problems they are having with a guy usually talk to other teenagers—who themselves are also limited in experience and knowledge. Sexual abuse in teen relationships can involve overt behavior: forced sexual intercourse, coercing the girl into viewing or acting out situations that she considers pornographic or otherwise objectionable, date rape, statutory rape (check the laws in your state regarding age of consent), leering at a female's sexual body parts, unwanted kissing, unwanted touching. Less overt actions can be equally damaging and offensive. Bear in mind, sexual abuse tactics, whether overt or subtle, are not about love or passion; they are about boys establishing and maintaining power and control over their female partners.

Brenda's Story

Remaining a virgin until marriage was very important to Brenda. "I was trying to do good, to do the right thing," the twenty-seven-year-old Christian woman recalls, looking back on the one-year relationship she had with a man named Martin when she was nineteen. "I enjoyed being intimate with Martin: the cuddling, kissing, and all that stuff. But my own principles and values told me I should wait to have sex until after I was married."

From the beginning, Brenda says, her boyfriend wanted far more sexually than she was willing to give. "He would always tell me 'Oh, this is so hard; I can barely stand it. Guys have to have sex. I need you so badly. Since we're going to marry anyway, then why wait?'" The young woman was aware of the pressure welling inside her. "Each time we'd fool around, Martin would apply new tactics that took us a step closer to having intercourse," Brenda says. "When I would say no to any of his advances, he would imply that I was being a tease. Or he'd say he simply wanted to teach me the many ways I could please him. And, one of his most effective tactics was to say 'I love you.' Like most females, I was especially vulnerable to this form of control. I mean, what girl or woman doesn't want to be loved or to please the guy in her life?"

Buckling under her boyfriend's constant sexual pressure, Brenda now realizes she was used. "After Martin and I started having sex, I began to see a pattern: he'd say 'I love you' and 'I need you' to get whatever he wanted from me. Martin's definition of love and need were based upon the popular media description. You know, this kind of romantic drama where females compromise who they are and what they believe in order to please their men. It's the woman's responsibility, we are told, to make men happy sexually, and in all other regards. So I gave up who I was instead of having a mate who supported where I was at and what I believed. Martin had convinced me his happiness was up to me. And I bought into his unhealthy and false belief system. As a result, I nearly had the life sucked out of me."

One other point must be made about the sexual abuse tactics employed by teen boys upon their intimate female partners. Over the years, many teenage girls and young women have said that they eventually yielded to the sexual pressure put on them by their boyfriends and other males because, as Martin proclaimed to Brenda, guys "have to have sex." Take it from a man, this often used (and, unfortunately, highly successful) line is, to be blunt, an absolute lie! It is always wrong for anyone to force another person (male or female) to do what they do not want to do, sexually or otherwise. To all teenage girls: never buy into the lie that boys "have to have sex."

Physical Abuse

At the time of our interview, Michael Fukuda was the community programs social work manager for the Queen Emma Clinics at The Queen's Medical Center in Honolulu. A mature Christian and longtime advocate working for the prevention and eradication of abusive and violent teen relationships, Fukuda is amazed at what he often witnesses when he arrives on high school campuses throughout various parts of Oahu. "I'll actually observe episodes of physical, psychological, and verbal abuse," he says. Fukuda notes that his close encounters are in no way happenstance or isolated. "Clearly, I stand out. The students know I'm not a teacher, and some of them even know me as 'that guy from Queen's who speaks about dating violence.' So, you would expect them to be on their best behavior. Nevertheless, I've witnessed firsthand, on a number of occasions and in the presence of their peers, boys grabbing, restraining, and forcing girls to do things these girls would rather not be doing. And, as we know, by the time physical aspects of abuse appear, there have already been many other episodes of hurt, on an emotional, verbal, sexual, and psychological level. But many teens don't even recognize these behaviors as abusive."

As Fukuda accurately points out, physical abuse is usually a later tactic used by male perpetrators of teen dating and teen relationship violence. When all other tactics—incessant pages and phone calls, subtle and overt putdowns, threats to pets and property, sexual degradation, humiliation, and pressure—no longer work or begin to lose their effectiveness, boys sometimes turn to making threats of and even carrying out acts of physical violence. Recall the words of Rodney Kahao, a former perpetrator of teen relationship violence, on pages 89-90. When the verbal, emotional, and sexual abuse tactics he used against his girlfriend were no longer effective, he turned to a tactic that he says always worked: "I began to beat her."

Dr. Jill Murray writes:

> It is widely accepted by those researching domestic violence—of which dating violence is a subhead—that there are certain undeniable possible effects of physical abuse on women and girls:
> • death by suicide
> • death by homicide
> • disabling injuries
> • depression
> • difficulty in obtaining, maintaining, and adjusting to employment

- emotional abuse and deprivation
- social isolation by the abuser
- escalation of violence
- loss of self-esteem
- sense of hopelessness and powerlessness
- sense of shame and guilt
- sense of loss of identity
- undermining of a sense of sanity and competence
- breakdown of coping skills
- high risk for alcoholism and drug use[5]

Having laid out some of the behaviors that constitute teen dating and teen relationship violence, let us now focus our attention on how Christians can become more attuned to warning signs that a teenage girl is being violated by her boyfriend or any other male.

Warning Signs

Barrie Levy is a pioneer in the field of teen relationship violence. She began her work in the mid-1970s and has authored four books, including the seminal work *Dating Violence: Young Women in Danger,* and a book for teens titled *In Love and In Danger: A Teen's Guide to Breaking Free of Abusive Relationships* (published by Seal Press in 1991 and 1998, respectively). In addition, Levy put together a curriculum to help schools educate adolescents about teen relationship violence. She has also trained teachers and others to use these materials to identify teen relationship violence and to perform crisis intervention. I asked Levy to discuss what parents and other adults need to look for regarding teen dating and teen relationship violence.

"Adults need to pay attention to anything that would make them concerned that this young person is different, that she has changed in some way," Levy explains. "Somebody, for example, who was very active and had a lot of friends, but who is suddenly more isolated and cutting off friendships. They used to be more motivated in school, but now show little or no interest in academics. These changes in behavior could be a reaction to having a jealous boyfriend. The jealousy rapidly becomes controlling, critical, manipulative, explosive, or violent behavior." Levy also described a multiplicity of other behaviors that may indicate that a young person is in danger. She talked specifically about girls who begin restricting themselves.

"Parents may begin to notice their daughter is afraid to do things that her boyfriend will either disapprove of or will be angry about. They may observe that he calls constantly to check up on her or that he has an explosive temper. For instance, they observe that she's afraid to spend time with her friends because that's going to make her boyfriend mad. Also, a daughter who has been active and done things in her life she feels good about suddenly feels bad about them. For example, she enjoys being a cheerleader, but she quits the squad because 'Danny says only sluts do that.' There have been so many girls I've worked with who have dropped activities they've enjoyed, or dropped out of school altogether, because of their boyfriend's jealousy and fear of his temper. 'He thinks I'm going to be talking to other guys so he won't let me go.' Or 'He only wants me to spend time with him—and he's cutting classes—so I have to cut, too.' Sometimes, the young person willingly leaves school or drops activities because she wants to be with her boyfriend. Girls may feel contradictory responses, feeling restricted and controlled and also feeling her boyfriend's restrictions as signs of love. A girl might say, 'He cares so much about me that he only wants me all to himself and to be with me.' This isn't healthy."

Levy also stresses the importance of sensitivity by parents and other adults to girls with unexplained injuries; girls who seem fearful of, or isolated by, their boyfriends; and girls receiving incessant phone calls and pages. "Some of the first signs parents get that their daughters may be in trouble are physical injuries or signs that their daughters are afraid of their boyfriends," Levy says. "If you see signs that your daughter is possibly ashamed or is being shamed, is dressing in baggy clothes, doesn't seem to care about her appearance, overreacts to being touched, displays a lack of concentration, and is experiencing either sleeplessness or nightmares, then be on alert: her boyfriend may be sexually abusing her."

Lorena described warning signs of abuse from the perspective of a survivor of teen relationship violence. She cautioned parents and all other adults to watch for signs of rapid changes in their daughters, to be concerned if their daughters are receiving incessant phone calls and pages, and to take heed if their daughters are involved with males who attempt to either isolate them or act out of intense jealousy. Addressing teens directly, Lorena points out, "If you have to adjust yourself in any way, shape, or form just to accommodate another person, that's a huge red flag. No one should have to be any way other than themselves. So be especially cautious if anyone is asking you to change the way you dress, the way you act, the way you talk, and so forth." And teens, says Lorena, should not be overly-concerned with what she terms "deep intimacy." "You don't have to find your soul mate in junior high or high school. Instead, spend time discovering who you are."

Spiritual and Emotional Effects

The spiritual and emotional effects of dating and relationship violence, both on the violated teenager and her parents, can be profound and lingering. Issues that often must be faced include: wrestling with why a loving God did not protect the victim from the violence or did not intervene in stopping the abuse; a loss of trust in God, Christ, other people, prayer, worship, and in oneself; and the tendency on the part of survivors to blame and belittle themselves. These issues are intensified by the all-too-common and inadequate responses offered to survivors and parents by well-intentioned but undertrained Christian clergy and laity. As a result, many teen victims are afraid to disclose abuse to churchgoers. Survivors also fear they will be judged. "Over the years, many teens have said to me that they wouldn't talk to anyone in the church about the violence they're experiencing because they expect church members to judge them about dating and, also, about sex," says

Barrie Levy. "The teens have told me that people from the church are going to tell them what they are doing is sinful. So if teens are having problems in their relationships, they think they're not going to be listened to, or they're not going to receive good advice from church members."

In the next chapter, we will look at the many ways Christians can provide compassionate and sensitive care to victims of teen dating and teen relationship violence, help the boys who perpetrate this sin, and better assist parents. First, we must explore the anger many teen survivors and their parents feel toward God. Survivors who feel anger toward God because of episodes of dating and relationship violence need to be able to express their anger without being made to feel guilty or ashamed. Christians need to understand that anger is a normal and healthy response to losing someone or something valuable to us. Situations of dating and relationship violence rob the victimized teen of what ought to be a fun and carefree time of life. These inappropriate actions take away a survivor's innocence and often compromise the faith, love, and trust she and her parents have in God, Christ, humanity, and in themselves.

While not all victims and parents experience anger at God, many will feel this way at someone or something during the long and difficult process of returning to wholeness. Expressing anger helps people move into therapeutic grieving and healing. Unfortunately, sometimes our own anxieties and personal, religious, or spiritual beliefs stifle our ability to listen supportively to another's anger. Many of us feel the need to defend or justify God when God is the target of a person's anger, but to do so discounts his or her feelings.[6] Christians must allow survivors and parents, in a nonjudgmental way, to express what they are feeling and to refrain from coming to the defense of God.

What are some of the spiritual and emotional struggles that survivors of teen dating and teen relationship violence face? How do the parents of a teenage daughter who was murdered by an abusive teenage boyfriend cope with this tragic loss, spiritually and emotionally? As we listen to the stories told by two young women who survived episodes of abuse during their teen years, and to the story of parents whose teenage daughter did not survive the violence, let all of us as Christians commit ourselves to seeking ways to provide more effective spiritual and emotional care to both victims and their parents.

Christie Corpuz's Story II

The spiritual and emotional scars suffered by Christie Corpuz from years of child abuse and teen dating violence are buried deep inside her. But sometimes her words reveal them. "My faith is slowly returning," the twenty-six-year-old Christian survivor says. "In October 1999, our church had a month of prayer. Normally, whenever there are prayer meetings or evangelists visiting, I stay away; I'm so afraid that other people are going to see right through me and know that I'm just playing church. But, at the encouragement of my mom, I accompanied her to the meeting. We were seated at the back of the sanctuary." Initially, Christie says, she did not think she would be able to remain at the prayer meeting. "I could feel my spirit being stirred. I told myself I needed to leave because I didn't want the pastor and parishioners to see me cry. My fear was if I cried then I would lose control; to me, this would mean that I was weak."

But, despite her fears, Christie stayed at the meeting. Forming a circle with the other congregants, Christie found herself overwhelmed with emotion. "I was getting an asthmatic attack because I was crying so hard," Christie said. The pastor's wife approached her and offered advice that Christie found very helpful: she suggested that the beleaguered young woman turn her burdens over to God. Then she asked Christie a question. "She wanted to know if I hated God. I said I didn't know if I hated God or if I loved God. The pastor's wife then started to pray, and she asked me to repeat after her. This was real helpful because I truly felt that I no longer knew how to pray on my own."

Following this prayer meeting, Christie says she felt some of the burdens from her long history of abuse lifted. "I remember repeating what the minister's wife had prayed and, afterwards, feeling so light," Christie says. "Normally, I struggle to get even two hours of restless sleep a night. But on that night, I actually went to bed at 10:00 PM and didn't wake up until around 7:00 the next morning. It was the first time I had a full night of sleep in as long as I could remember. So, little by little, I'm gaining trust again in God."

Lorena's Story II

Twenty-two-year-old Lorena says her relationship with God is a struggle. "I still believe in God," this survivor says. "But the abuse I suffered as a teenager has had a huge effect on my spirituality." Lorena has a very difficult time understanding God's lack of support during her many hours of need. "I wonder why God allowed me to go through so much, for so long," the young woman laments. "Why, for instance, didn't God help me break free sooner? How come God allowed my life to be in such danger?" Lorena says she is all the more baffled by God's silence during those many times she begged for God's mercy. "I would always plead with God to please help me change my boyfriend. I now realize it is not my job to change anybody. Nevertheless, at the time I was going through so much pain, I do remember having strong negative and hostile feelings toward God. The abuse was such an awful experience, and I kept wondering how come I was left all by myself."

Lorena remains in a state of spiritual and emotional uncertainty. "Even though I have no bruises or scars, my memories are still with me. All of the hurt of being in such a violent relationship, and without the support of God or other people, is still with me. It's something I'll carry throughout my life and, through my creative work with Interval House, I am learning how to positively deal with these memories."

Elsa and Jim Croucher's Story

Visiting Elsa and Jim Croucher is like visiting loving grandparents for dinner on a Sunday afternoon—the Crouchers are open, joyous, and peaceful. This was clearly evident the day the couple conversed with two dozen or so other Christians, both clergy and laity, at a domestic violence training event I led in Anderson, Indiana, in June 2000. Like all the other participants, the Crouchers displayed a wide range of emotions during our eight hours together. They cried, grimaced, groaned, and raged as stories were told about and by victims and survivors of domestic violence, especially when the abused women were either blamed or not believed after they disclosed their stories to pastors and parishioners. And, along with everyone else, Jim and Elsa worked diligently, in small and large groups, to discover ways to prevent and eradicate the abuse that is so prevalent in society, including among Christians. In addition, during lighter moments, the Crouchers joked and laughed with their Christian sisters and brothers.

What was not evident to attendees at the Anderson conference as they gazed into Elsa's and Jim's warm eyes are the spiritual and emotional scars the couple must carry with them at all times—scars caused by the murder of their youngest child, Tina, by her boyfriend. "I had left work early that day because I kept calling the house and no one answered," Elsa says, thinking back to December 21, 1992, the day Tina was shot to death while she lay sleeping in her bed. "I knew something was wrong. And, when I arrived home, there were police cars lined up on our street. The coroner's car was also there. As I pulled up in front of my house, they were rolling a body out. That was my greeting home."

How do Christian parents cope with the spiritual and emotional devastation caused by the murder of their child? What are the most helpful ways clergy and churchgoers can comfort and support a bereaved mother and father? What warning signs should Christians heed concerning teen dating and teen relationship violence? Let us listen as Jim and Elsa Croucher share their story with us.

A hardworking couple who had already put their three oldest children through college, the Crouchers spoke often about what they would do after their youngest child completed her higher education. "Our grand plan was to finish thirty years at our jobs and retire," says Jim. "We moved to a three-bedroom house from our five-bedroom home. This move was a nice one for Elsa, Tina, and myself. When Tina finished college, Elsa and I planned to stay in that house for the rest of our lives. Everything was supposed to come together as we had so often discussed: our daughter would graduate from college, Elsa and I would be retiring, and our house would just about be paid for."

Tina's murder changed all those plans. Her parents never slept another night in their new home. "We just couldn't do it," Elsa says. "We stayed there during the day because it was where everyone gathered. But, at night, we just couldn't bear the thought of sleeping in the same house where our daughter had been murdered." The Crouchers were made an offer by another couple that overwhelmed them. "They were only acquaintances," says Elsa, "and had just moved from a big house, which was up for sale, into a smaller home. Well, the couple sent word by their son, who was a friend of our children, that we could stay in their big house for as long as we needed. All we had to do was to pay utilities. This was sure very gracious of them. We ended up staying there four months."

The Crouchers found it extremely difficult to concentrate in the wake of their daughter's death. They attempted to ease their sorrow by throwing themselves into their work, but discovered they simply could not function. "Depression was so bad we could hardly look at any teenage girl without crying," Jim says. "We could not keep our minds on anything." Elsa described the initial numbing effect of her grief. "It was like I had no feeling," she recalls. "I just went through the actions, doing what I had to do as days went by." Unable to concentrate on their jobs, both Jim and Elsa were forced to take early retirement.

Dedicated Christians for decades, the Crouchers' faith had been abruptly challenged. "I have been a Christian since I was a child," says Elsa, whose father was an ordained minister. "But after Tina was killed, for the first time in my life I wondered about God. I wondered, how on earth could he allow something like this to happen? Something so senseless, so devastating." Jim had one question for God. "My big question was 'Why, God? Why?' I was very angry at God, and it took me many, many months before I could pray again." Eventually, Jim turned back to God, and to his church, to find refuge for his shattered soul. "I started to realize that God, in his wisdom, was taking care of us," he says. "And, slowly, my faith in God began to return. My wife and I grew closer together, I think, because we needed each other so much. But, without the Lord's help, and the help of our Christian family who gave us all the support they did, I don't believe Elsa and I would have made it as a couple."

The death of a child—under any circumstances—challenges all those who come into contact with the grieving parents. Well-meaning people often offer trite statements intended to give comfort. Jim and Elsa Croucher found such platitudes unhelpful, even harmful. Still, the bereaved couple expressed appreciation to all people who reached out to them. "Their intentions were good," Elsa says. "But they would have been far better off just walking up, putting their arms around us, and saying nothing. Or, if they had said, 'I'm sorry for your loss,' or, 'I'm here for you.'" Jim agrees. "When you experience a tragedy such as ours," he said, "people want to say something that will bring comfort. But, sometimes, they just say the wrong things." The Crouchers were most troubled by suggestions that Tina's death was "God's will," and observations that it was simply "Tina's time to go" and that "God won't ever give you any more than you can bear."

The Crouchers took great comfort, however, in responses they received from the vast majority of people living in and around their hometown of Monroe, Ohio. "Most of our Christian friends rallied around us," says Elsa. "We were supported from the very day Tina was killed, and this support went on indefinitely. We had people visiting our home, people calling us on the phone, sending us notes, bringing us food, and we had people praying for us. The Christian folks throughout our community, and especially, those from our own congregation, just carried us."

In the years since Tina Croucher was murdered, her parents have turned this tragic event into a mission. They have established an organization dedicated to preventing acts of violence in both teen and adult intimate relationships (this organization will be discussed in detail in chapter 5). They share their story nationwide. The couple offers a particular message about teen dating and teen relationship violence to church folks. "A lot of Christians think that teen dating and teen relationship violence happens only outside the church community," Jim says. "But it occurs among kids in our congregations, too. For example, the young man who killed our daughter was at the altar a time or two, praying to the Lord. He was in the church's youth group as well. Yet, on youth trips, he slapped Tina on the bus. So Christians must open their eyes to the problem within their own community. We must also recognize that dating violence occurs in various social and economic groups. At our talks, we see kids whose parents are doctors, lawyers, and pastors. We have to be on the lookout for warning signs of abuse occurring among our teens, inside and outside of our parishes."

As part of their mission, Jim and Elsa Croucher point out warning signs that may indicate that a young person is in a dangerous relationship. "When we go into schools and churches, we tell kids that if they know of a friend who is being abused in any way, they need to tell somebody," Elsa says. "Kids need to let a counselor, nurse, teacher, principal, youth minister, and, most of all, a parent, know what's going on." One of the reasons that the Crouchers are so persistent in their quest for young people to disclose acts of teen abuse and violence is related to a statement made by many of the teenage girls who attended Tina's funeral. "The thing that came back to haunt us a year or so after our daughter's death was remembering all the young girls who came through the receiving line at the funeral home. Barely able to talk because they were sobbing so hard, the girls repeated the same phrase over and over to Elsa and me: 'We should have told you,' they cried, 'We should have told you.' They all knew Tina was in great danger, and because they never told us or any other adult about it, these young women are still carrying that guilt."

The Crouchers offer an equally strong message about warning signs to the parents of teenage girls. "Watch that your daughter's boyfriend doesn't try to control her," says Jim. "If your daughter starts changing the way she dresses, the way she wears her hair, or if she suddenly stops spending time with her friends, be concerned. This could indicate that the boy is controlling or isolating your daughter. Also, if the boy calls often and questions what your daughter is doing, where she's been or going, and who your daughter is talking to, this is a red flag." He also warns, "Look for any changes in your daughter's personality. When Tina was dating the young man who ended up murdering her, her personality was completely soured. She developed an overall bad attitude, was angry at everybody, and snapped at people all the time. Elsa and I could tell the very day she broke up with him. Tina immediately returned to being our bubbly, loving daughter."

Conclusion

For teens in and out of the church, acts of abuse and violence perpetrated by teenage boys against teenage girls occur far more frequently than most adults may acknowledge or imagine. This widespread problem will not go away if we deny its prevalence. In fact, if we choose to be uninformed, we are doing a great injustice to both our daughters and our sons. As Christians, we must face the reality that among our own teens there are girls living in horror because of emotional, verbal, sexual, and physical abuse they are suffering at the hands of boys.

Spiritual leaders and parishioners have to make the commitment to educate themselves on the various tactics teen boys use to gain power and control over teen girls, and about the messages we send teen boys that seem to give them permission to do so. We must also be open to learning the myriad warning signs that may indicate our teenage daughters are experiencing abuse or the potential for abuse. In addition, Christians must have a clear understanding of the harsh and lingering effects abuse and violence have upon the spiritual and emotional state of our daughters. In and out of church, we can be a very positive influence upon all young people involved in dating and relationship violence. To meet this challenge, however, we must first take the steps that will prepare us to approach these complicated situations.

Questions for Discussion

1. Name and discuss at least five behaviors that constitute teen dating and teen relationship violence.
2. What did you feel after reading Tina's story? How would you offer support to Elsa and Jim Croucher after their daughter was murdered?
3. Name and discuss at least five warning signs that may indicate a teenage girl is being abused by her boyfriend or another male teen.
4. What are at least five negative effects dating or relationship violence have upon the spiritual and emotional state of victimized teenage girls? In your Christian beliefs, is it acceptable for people to express anger at God? Elaborate.
5. Are there girls and boys in the church you attend who are either being victimized by, or are the victimizers of, other teens? What are you yourself doing in an attempt to intervene? Have you discussed this situation with anyone else? If so, how did that person respond?

4.

Teen Dating and Relationship Violence: Prevention and Intervention

How can Christians help prevent violence in teen dating and teen relationships? When should we begin addressing these issues with our daughters and sons, and in our places of worship? What are the do's and don'ts regarding intervention?

A Christian Young Man Speaks Out: Bryant Chandler

At the time of our interview, Bryant Chandler was sixteen and a few months away from beginning his senior year at a suburban public high school in San Antonio, Texas. Raised in a Christian home, the tall, lanky young man struggles with the abusive and sexist behavior he regularly sees his male peers inflict on teenage girls. I asked Bryant about his observations and to discuss the role his Christian faith and upbringing plays in keeping him from following his peers' lead.

"Guys don't value women in any way, any more," Bryant says. "At my school, boys just brag on what they're doing to girls sexually. And if the girls have an attitude, these guys call them 'bitches.' If the girls have a lot of male friends, the guys call them 'hoes.' But it's the boys themselves who are looking for a way to use the girls sexually, then leave them. It's the guys who are bragging about how many girls they've had sex with; it's the guys who talk about how they don't like girls, they just use them for sex; it's the guys who say they won't buy girls anything or take them out; and it's the guys who cheat on the girls. So, why are these guys calling girls 'hoes'?"

Bryant, who is African American, says at first he noticed the abusive and sexist attitudes coming only from the boys of his own race. "It used to be mostly in the black culture where I'd hear a lot of boys refer to girls as 'bitches' and 'hoes'," the young man says. "But now I hear guys from all cultures use these words to refer to women and girls. They don't even see the terms as wrong any more. Guys use 'bitch' and 'ho' as though that's what females are supposed to be called. It's like one of the main things you hear nowadays—if I'm talking with a friend and we see a girl coming down the hall, he'll say 'Oh, don't talk to her, she's so and so's bitch. You better leave her alone.'"

Bryant says the abusive language is in no way toned down when teachers are present. "Oh yeah, boys say these words in front of anyone," he insists. "It's not like guys look around first to see if teachers are there. It's just normal speech to these guys."

Bryant is especially disturbed by a situation of physical violence he recently witnessed in his school's cafeteria. "We were all eating lunch, and this guy and girl who had, I guess, been dating for a while were there also. Well, the guy was embarrassed by something the girl said and, in front of the whole cafeteria, he punched her in the face with his fist. We were all shocked. And the guy didn't even get in that much trouble. He spent a week in Alternative School for disciplinary action, and that was it. Then he was allowed to come back. The incident was never even talked about by our teachers with the rest of us."

How has Bryant managed to avoid the pitfalls of abuse and violence that seem to plague so many of his male peers? What messages has he received over the years from his parents concerning how he should treat others, girls and boys alike? What does this young man have to offer other Christian teens about behaving appropriately toward one another?

"My parents brought me up, I think, exactly how they should have," Bryant explains. "The Bible was pretty much what they based their upbringing on. I was always taught wrong from right, to do unto others as I would want others to do unto me, and to look at what Jesus would do if he were in the same situation. It's pretty easy really to tell what's wrong from what is right by simply using common sense. My parents just wanted me to understand these basic principles, so that I could make the right decisions."

According to Bryant, his parents also gave him instructions regarding how he was to treat other individuals. "They told me over and over again that it was never right to try to control what another person did or thought. If I didn't like being controlled, they said, then I shouldn't try to control anyone else." In addition, Bryant remembers specific lessons he received from his father and mother about being a male. "I was always taught that when I do get a partner I need to treat her as my equal, to never see myself as on a higher plane than she is. I don't know the exact chapter and verse, but the Bible does talk about treating your wife as an equal; that in no way should a husband control or put his wife down."

Bryant recently began applying his parents' lessons about egalitarian and nonabusive behavior in his own dating relationship. "We're treating each other pretty good," Bryant says. The two teens work hard at maintaining healthy boundaries. "Just this past week, my girlfriend was telling me how she's bored because of all the hours I've been working. She told me about this other guy that liked her and she asked, 'What if I go to the movies with him?' I told her, 'You don't have to ask me to go out with someone else. That's up to you. I'm not going to try and control what you do.'"

If his girlfriend did in fact go out with another guy "it would hurt," Bryant admits. "But I don't want to try and control what she does. And this is the same way she treats me." He cites as an example those weekends that he wants to spend time with his friends, while his girlfriend desires time alone with him. "Even though she'd rather I'd be with her, she never tells me what I can and cannot do," he says. "We both understand that attempting to control someone else is always wrong."

Bryant continues to learn the importance of setting limits. "I think in relationships between Christian teenagers there have to be certain boundaries," he says. "We don't have to know every single thing that the other person is doing. For a relationship to work, Christian teenagers need to get to know each other very well. There needs to also be a lot of communication. If you don't like what a person is doing, or if something is being done that seems abusive or wrong, then you need to tell the other person, or tell someone else who can help you deal with the situation."

In addition to the many lessons he's learned from his parents, Bryant says, his faith in Jesus Christ is helping him to stay on a healthy path. "It's really easy to get lost in worldly stuff," he says. "If I'm not grounded in my faith, I could end up involved in things that aren't right for me: alcohol, drugs, sex, abuse. Temptation surrounds me every day. And there's always something that people want me to do that isn't right. I have to stay strong in my Christian faith to keep doing the right thing."

Violence Prevention: Start Early, Repeat Often

Our children probably won't reap the full benefit of our teachings about violence prevention if we, as a faith community, wait until young people reach puberty before we begin addressing the problem. We need to begin these lessons very early in the lives of our children. Violence prevention needs to be discussed on a regular basis by all Christians.

"Our kids are so eager to please that it's easy to teach them the right things to do, as well as the wrong things," says Barbara Chandler, a social worker whose clients have witnessed and experienced violence perpetrated by a household member. She works for the San Antonio Child Guidance Center, an outpatient mental health center for children between the ages of three and eighteen and their families.

"In articles, books, newspapers, and the stories we watch on television, it's easy to point out negative behavior to children, to raise their consciousness," Chandler says. She contended that the earlier we offer our daughters and sons information containing alternatives to violence, the better chances we have to live in a violence-free world. "It's beneficial to use teachable moments to educate our children. By doing this, we can teach our kids self-respect, how to treat other people, and basic social skills regarding what's appropriate and what's not appropriate—even at a very, very young age. Prevention also requires us to tell our children that there are people who will and can abuse them, and that it's not acceptable. We must impress upon our children that they do not have to accept this abuse or subject themselves to any other kind of inappropriate actions.

"The Bible gives us the framework for what we are to expect. We are children of the king, and, as such, we come from a royal heritage," Chandler says. "Therefore, we need to bring up our children with an awareness of this fact. Abuse is not the way to treat anyone, especially descendants of royalty. We must let our children know to carry their heads high, and that they deserve the best from people. If they're not getting this type of respect, then our children need to put distance between themselves and these unhealthy relationships."

Chandler is not only a devout Christian and a counselor with years of experience, she is also the mother of Bryant, the sixteen-year-old young man whose story opened this chapter.

What lessons has she tried to instill in her son about violence prevention?

"Bryant's father and I have tried to model Christ-like principles in our relationship by demonstrating to our son mutual love and respect, and a willingness to compromise with each other," Barbara explains. She stresses that modeling should begin when a child is still a baby. "From the time he was an infant, Bryant was exposed to our Christian values. As he got older, we needed to help him understand it's never good to treat people in negative ways. For example, we let Bryant know it's not acceptable behavior to hit other people, male or female, not even to get what he wants or in an attempt to control someone. Both his dad and I stressed the importance of treating everyone with respect. We also encouraged our son, from a very early age, to find appropriate ways to meet his needs, instead of using abusive and violent tactics."

Chandler says she and her husband also made it clear to Bryant to always respect the boundaries of other people. "We told our son, 'You don't force people to do things they don't want to do.' And we helped him to understand that if someone tells him 'no,' regardless of the circumstances, then he needs to accept their 'no.'"

Chandler is cautiously optimistic that the many lessons she and her husband have taught their son for all of his sixteen years are being internalized. "I hope and pray that all we've said is sinking in, and that these teachings will be a guiding force for Bryant in his relationship with females, and that he has learned to treat everyone with respect. I believe we have given him a good foundation. And I can already see how our lessons are being positively played out in his relationships with me, his dad, his younger sister, and other people."

Chandler insists violence prevention must begin at home, and that it has to always be addressed candidly. "Christian parents can't assume this issue is going to be taken on by the school and, unfortunately, we can't assume that our churches will deal with the problem either. If we don't talk about violence prevention, our children are not going to deal with the issue through osmosis. Therefore, we

Christians need to be more proactive in helping our kids deal with their problems in nonabusive ways."

Modeling Healthy Responses to Conflict

A snippet of faded and heavily scratched Super 8MM film, which was shot in the summer of 1968, shows my fifty-one-year-old father dancing with my forty-two-year-old mother on the patio of our home. Smiling brightly and eyeing one another with looks of playful arrogance, my parents attempt to outdo one another by offering their own unique renditions of the Stroll, the Twist, and a few other unrecognizable dances from that era. Moments before the film abruptly ends, Daddy comes up from behind Mama and kisses her softly on the cheek.

This tender and warm piece of silent history captures, in less than a half minute, my parents' twenty-five-year marriage. They were each other's best friend, spending most of the limited amount of free time they had with their four children, and with one another, laughing and talking. It's been many years since they died, and yet I still have sacred images from their relationship: hearing them laugh and talk with each other in bed on Saturday mornings; watching Daddy embrace Mama and affectionately pat her on the bottom when he would arrive home from work; and seeing them gently hold hands on the way to church. The behavior my parents manifested with one another offered me a healthy model that I employ in my own marriage—showing my wife the love, respect, and tenderness that all humans deserve.

Equally important for my transition from boyhood to becoming a man, however, was how my parents modeled for me healthy responses to the many conflicts that arose between them. Like all humans, especially those in long-term intimate relationships, my mother and father had their share of disagreements. The focus of their conflicts usually centered on how they should and should not spend their meager finances. But even though Daddy and Mama differed widely on what goods and services they considered to be necessary, they didn't abuse or violate one another in any way.

The greatest lesson I learned regarding appropriate responses to conflict came from my father. When an argument between him and Mama would escalate, he would literally turn and walk away. Somehow, my father understood the value of taking a "time out" long before this approach was even conceptualized. In my late teens, shortly before his death, I asked Daddy about this. "I walk away from your mother because I never want to say or do anything to her that I will later regret," my father said. His simple explanation has had a great impact on how I deal with conflict—both in and out of my marriage. Acts of abuse and violence, I learned from Daddy, are never appropriate responses to working out disagreements.

To me, it is very important for all Christian couples to model for our children healthy responses to the conflicts that inevitably occur within marriages and other intimate partnerships. Otherwise, our children will not know what to do when disagreements arise. Jerry Coffee, who for many years has worked on Oahu developing violence and substance abuse prevention curricula for teenagers and younger children, cautions parents about trying to shield their disagreements from their children. "One of the things I tell adults when I'm doing a violence prevention piece is that if we go behind a curtain when we argue, like the wizard did in *The Wizard of Oz,* then our kids will grow up thinking that conflict doesn't happen or that people don't disagree," Coffee says. "So when conflict does happen in their lives, these young people are ill-prepared to deal with it. What they generally do is nothing—continuously building up residual anger until the person snaps."

Coffee believes children can learn positive ways to deal with conflict through modeling and mediation. "We need to teach our kids how to be present with their anger, so that they're not stuffing it," he says. "I know a lot of parents struggle with how to best do this, and I myself struggle with that in my own marriage, but we must find ways to help our kids."

Paul Kivel, a violence-prevention educator, has many insights into how parents can model for children nonviolent approaches to conflict. He is a nationally known expert on men's issues and the cofounder of the Oakland Men's Project, which helps men confront and change violent behavior. In his landmark book *Men's Work*, Kivel speaks directly to parents out of his own experience:

> Our children never intentionally hurt each other or try to destroy anything unless they're feeling angry and powerless and violence is the only way they think they can get it back. Even then, as parents, we don't allow them to hurt others, although we may understand the frustration and pain that led to the anger.

In our home we start out with some simple, clear rules:
- No hitting, kicking, biting, or hurting others, including the animals and plants around us.
- No kissing, hugging, touching, or other contact with a person who does not want it.
- No teasing or name-calling.
- No throwing things in the house or at people; no threats or intimidation.

These rules apply even to the babies. There are explanations provided as the children grow old enough to talk, but the limits on violence come first. The rules apply to the adults. We are not allowed to do any of these things, even in retaliation for children breaking the rules.

Our children understand the importance of these rules because they can feel the danger from adults and adult anger. They don't always have the control to stop themselves, and sometimes they have no other way to express their anger, unless and until we teach them. So they do break the rules sometimes and hit, tease, or call each other names. They are given a time-out, a chance to sit quietly by themselves and think about what they did. If they do not voluntarily go into another room to take the time-out, my partner or I will pick them up, gently but firmly, and carry them to their room.

Before the time-out is over we talk with them about whatever feelings remain from the event.[1]

Helping Our Sons Unlearn Inappropriate Lessons

All humans are capable of violence. It is learned behavior that has, unfortunately, been passed on in an intergenerational fashion since the beginning of humankind. Therefore, we need to learn alternatives to this destructive teaching. The lessons promoted earlier in the chapter by Barbara Chandler, Jerry Coffee, and Paul Kivel help us to realize our goal. It is important to teach our sons and daughters to respond to other people in a loving and respectful manner.

Because boys most often receive unhealthy teachings about what it means to be male, we need to help them unlearn several inappropriate lessons. A discussion of three of the lessons follows.

Expressing Anger with Violence

"My girlfriend made me angry, that's why I beat her up." "I was angry at the neighbor's dog. He wouldn't stop barking, so I crushed his skull with a brick." "My classmates made me angry because they wouldn't stop teasing me, so I shot them." These are some of the justifications boys use to explain and excuse acts of violence. From whom do they learn these inappropriate validations? They learn from parents, teachers, pastors, churchgoers, and society in general.

"We must tell kids that violence is an inappropriate response to our anger," Jerry Coffee says. "Anger is a secondary emotion; normally we experience other feelings, such as sadness or hurt, before we experience anger. But kids haven't had many role models helping them to learn how to express sadness and hurt. Unfortunately, a lot of role models in our culture are showing kids how to express anger through violence. Kids don't have their moral development completed, so they don't think about the consequences of their actions. All they are thinking about is relieving the symptoms of their anger. Pounding something, cursing someone, and screaming and yelling at people are good ways, kids think, to relieve feelings they would otherwise repress."

Even Christian parents excuse or justify violent behavior that boys use against other teens, adults, pets, and property. Many mothers and fathers over the years have offered a plain and straightforward reason why their son turned to violence: "He was angry." As Christians, we must teach our sons (and daughters) that anger is a feeling, while violence is a behavior. All of us have a right to our feelings, but none of us has a right to use abusive and violent behavior. These actions are always inexcusable and unacceptable.

Male Privilege
"Boys will be boys." "Boys have a right to use girls for sex." "Men are superior to women." "That's just the way males are." These are a few of the countless phrases used in our culture to excuse inappropriate male behavior. When we teach our sons that they can do whatever they want, especially to girls, and when we tell our boys there are no consequences for their behavior—even when the behavior abuses and violates others—we do a horrible disservice not only to the people (or pets and property) these boys hurt, but also to the boys themselves. Male privilege prevents boys (and men) from realizing the full potential of living in a healthy and egalitarian society. It also ensures that another generation will suffer under the abuse perpetrated by men and boys.

"I never had anybody teach me how to treat girls," confesses David Garcia, a former perpetrator of teen relationship violence and now a certified domestic violence counselor with the state of California and a teen advocate at Interval House. Now twenty-two, David grew up watching his father abuse his mother. "The only male role models I had were the ones nobody would want in the first place," David says. "Obviously, this was a problem when I started dating."

In addition to his abusive father, David speaks candidly about the inappropriate messages he received from older boys regarding how to treat girls. "The guys gave me a lot of information that you wouldn't want anybody to have. The biggest thing they kept encouraging me to do was to try and get as far as I possibly could with girls sexually. Females were something to be used, these guys taught me; objects for a guy's sexual gratification. The concern was always the same: 'Where did you touch her?' 'Did you kiss her?' 'How far did you get with her?' There was never any talk from these guys about treating girls with respect; no conversation about emotional intimacy. These older boys weren't helpful in the least in preparing me for manhood. But the most unhealthy role model I had was my father, a wife beater and womanizer. Unfortunately, most of what I learned about how to treat females I learned from him."

Carole Sousa, an outreach coordinator for Transition House and cofounder of the Dating Violence Intervention Project (DVIP), a prevention education project to reach teenagers in Cambridge, Massachusetts, describes her organization's work with young men:

> Our approach with young men encourages them to reject stereotypical male roles. When we talk about ways men abuse power, we point out that we are not singling out any individual but that we are talking about a general problem. We say that at some point in his life every male will have to decide whether to use control and abuse over women: He will have to decide whether he will listen to a partner's "no" or push for what he wants. . . . The goal of our work with boys is to help them understand they have a variety of choices when dealing with relationship issues. Using violence is a choice. No one can "provoke" or make someone hit them. We try to build awareness about their choices and which ones lead to abuse. We discuss the legal consequences of choices such as rape or assault. We also discuss the real consequences in relationships that may be opposite to their intentions. For example, a boy who feels he uses abusive, jealous, or possessive behavior because he wants his girlfriend to understand how much she means to him actually pushes her away with this behavior. She may become more distant or become less honest with him in reaction to his accusations. We discuss alternative ways to show someone you care.[2]

The idea of male privilege guides our boys along the wrong path, encouraging them to conform to negative male role models. It compels young (and older) men to believe they have a right to whatever they want, no matter the consequences to other people or to themselves. And, perhaps most significantly for Christians, it robs boys of their right to become the type of individual God intends: kind and loving men who respect themselves and others.

Males Have a Special Place with God

The timeworn teaching that males have a special place with God was discussed at length in chapter 2. A further development of male privilege, the teaching needs to be unlearned by teenage boys (and adult men) because it contradicts the paramount values taught by God and Jesus Christ: equality, love, and respect for all of humankind. For centuries the Christian church has done an injustice to all people by propagating the false teaching that God and Christ somehow regard men and boys more favorably than women and girls. The emotional and spiritual damage suffered by Christian women and girls because of this skewed viewpoint has been catastrophic: males beat, curse, and rape females while claiming "God-given" authority as justification. We Christians must immediately end this form of spiritual abuse. Violence against women and girls cannot be prevented and will not be eradicated until we stop teaching men and boys the inaccurate concept that God favors males over females.

To Our Daughters: You Never Deserve to Be Abused

Violence prevention material that addresses teenage girls must always include the statement, "You never deserve to be abused!" This message is critical because many folks, even some from the religious community, believe there are circumstances that permit males to abuse females. Consider a few of the justifications offered by Christian women and men.

- "She has always dressed in a seductive way. I knew one day this would get her in trouble." (A Christian mother's comment after her daughter was raped by a male classmate.)
- "My daughter made a stupid choice. Look at what it got her." (A Christian father's remark after his teenage daughter was severely beaten by her boyfriend.)
- "I told her that guys are very jealous of their possessions. So she'd better stop provoking his anger." (A Christian mother's comment after her daughter was thrown out of a speeding car by her boyfriend. The perpetrator later confessed he committed the crime because the girl spent too much of their time together "smiling at other guys.")
- "He sure must have loved that little girl an awful lot." (A Christian grandmother speaking about her grandson; the young man had just murdered his eighteen-year-old former girlfriend.)

As we have seen, abuse is often an intergenerationally learned behavior. Girls who grow up watching their mothers being abused by husbands and boyfriends begin to consider the behavior normal. Recall the words of Christie Corpuz. Having grown up watching her father violate her mother, and, from age three, experiencing firsthand her father's criminal and sinful acts, Christie developed a very distorted worldview. Remember her comments from chapter 1: "As a child growing up, I thought abuse was normal. Anybody who didn't live in a home with violence, I told myself, must be from a weird family."

It is vital that parents speak out against all forms of violence and model nonabusive behaviors in our own intimate partnerships. "If your daughter was raised in a verbally, emotionally, or physically abusive household, she erroneously believes that *this is acceptable behavior*," writes Dr. Jill Murray.

Since you are her most important role model, as a mother you do not have the option of saying, "Your father treats me this way, but I want better for you." Or, as a father, "I am cruel to your mother. I say vicious things, treat her unbelievably poorly, and knock her around for her own good, but I'll kill a boy who does that to you." Obviously you see the ridiculousness of such comments. They are clearly hypocritical when paired with your actual behavior, and very confusing to a young girl experiencing a romantic relationship. Essentially, what you are saying is, "do as I say, not as I do."[3]

Barbara Chandler stresses the importance of the message that women deserve safety in relationships. "My contention has always been that when Christian women share information about being abused they need to hear the words, 'Abuse is not intended for you, no one deserves abuse, God wants better for you,'" she says. "It's not a matter of me telling women that they have to get out of their abusive relationship, or do anything else for that matter. The important message I try to offer all women is that they deserve to be safe, and that they need to take the steps to ensure their own safety. I inform these women that God loves them, and that God wants safety for themselves and for their daughters and sons."

Intervention: How Christians Can Help

Having looked at some ways to help prevent the common problems associated with teen dating and teen relationship violence, let us now turn our attention to how Christians can help intervene when the violence and associated problems are already present in the lives of our daughters and sons. As we proceed with this matter, it is important for us to remember never to attempt to conduct this intervention alone. Dealing with situations of violence involving teenagers can be very complicated. It requires a team of people, professionals and laity, working together. (We'll discuss the many ways churchgoers can partner with community service providers to address situations of teen dating and teen relationship violence and adult intimate partner abuse in the next chapter.)

In attempting to deal with abusive situations, church members must be careful to act within their level of training. An ideal starting point for clergy and lay people, therefore, is to seek education and training so they are better able to provide compassionate and sensitive support to teens who are being violated as well as to the young people who perpetrate this sin. Before spiritual leaders and parishioners can be helpful, they need to be able to identify and understand the complexities of the problem of abuse and violence in teen relationships. Taking action without proper training and understanding has the potential to cause more harm than good. (The resources section at the end of the book offers a list of agencies, books, and videos that will help inform Christians about this issue.)

"My desire is to see both teen relationship violence and domestic violence more openly discussed in churches," Barbara Chandler says. She reminds all people of faith about the example Christ set for us. "The church needs to take a leadership role in addressing these issues because, as Christians, it's not just us saying domestic violence and dating violence are wrong, but Christ also says treating others in abusive ways is wrong. So, in a very real sense, we're mandated to have a higher standard than what the world has."

Chandler is optimistic about the results of education given to Christians on teen relationship violence and adult intimate partner abuse awareness. "If the church is willing to look at these issues openly, it will send the message to all Christians that the congregation is a safe place to discuss our problems. As a result, this could help reduce incidents of abuse. Women and teenage girls might then receive a message from the entire church that they have choices: they don't have to stay in a relationship that is not safe or healthy for themselves and their children."

Victimized Teen Girls: Approaches To Intervention

Many teenagers distrust adults—even their own parents. They fear that adults will not listen to their viewpoints; that adults will judge them harshly for their choices (alcohol and drug use, selection of friends and intimate partners, decision to engage in sexual activities, etc.); and that adults will treat them like little children. It is unlikely that a teenage young woman who is being abused by her boyfriend or another male will look to adults for help. Teenage girls who do disclose abuse usually tell other teenagers, who are just as overwhelmed by the situation as the victimized young woman herself. Therefore, adult Christians must be very gentle and nonjudgmental when intervening in situations of reported abuse.

Barrie Levy, a pioneer in the field of teen dating violence awareness, offers this advice: "If you say, 'I don't like your boyfriend and I'm sick and tired of how much time you're spending with him,' that's not an opening—it shuts down the conversation." Levy encourages parents to exercise caution in their approach. "It's much more likely for a teenager to talk to another teenager about a relationship than it is for teens to talk to adults. So adults need to be responsible for initiating these conversations with teens, but not in a judgmental or frightening way."

Levy emphasizes the need for parents and other adults to show victimized teens their concern. "Adults might say to a teen, 'I'm worried about you. You haven't been yourself lately. You don't seem to care about your school work, and I know you're spending a lot of time with your boyfriend.' It's important that parents not only state what they observe with genuine concern and with some understanding, but it's also important that they remain open to getting a response from teens."

But what if our daughters deny there's a problem? Levy suggests that parents be persistent. "If your daughter says, 'No, there's nothing wrong, everything's fine,' you ask again. You don't just stop with one answer, especially if you see signs of abuse." (Refer to chapter 3 for more about the warnings that may indicate that a teenage girl is being victimized by her boyfriend or another male.) Levy says our gentle persistence sends a positive message to teenage girls facing peril. "The more open you are to hearing an answer, the greater likelihood there is that your daughter will open up to you. If she's troubled by how her boyfriend is treating her, and you show sincere concern, then your daughter will be less protective of the relationship and more likely to share."

Levy also points out an avenue leading to intervention that many parents might not consider. "I believe that parents sometimes overlook the access they have to sources of information about their kids," she says. "I don't mean secretive stuff; I'm talking about accessing open information, such as calling the school." The counselor explained how other people could provide vital information. "If you're worried about what's going on with your daughter, if there's a sudden change in her behavior, then other people may have heard or witnessed incidents about which you have no knowledge. So think of people at your daughter's school whom you can ask, 'Is she different at school?' 'How has she seemed there?' 'What do you notice?' Ask siblings and other relatives what they have heard or observed." Levy encourages all concerned citizens to resist the temptation to simply sit back and do nothing. "People tend to avoid facing these situations because they are uncomfortable to deal with. That type of response endangers a child even more."

Jerry Coffee also expresses the need for parents to be gentle and selective in how they approach their daughters about an abusive relationship. "The whole idea about picking and choosing your battles carefully becomes really important if you think that maybe your kid is in danger," he says. "Having a huge argument with your child over an unclean room or grades pales in comparison to your daughter's coming home with bruises on her body or hickeys all over her neck, or the fact that her boyfriend seems to be calling every ten minutes."

Coffee urges parents to be attentive to the quality of their relationships with their daughters in order to increase the possibility of having a positive influence in the midst of difficult circumstances. "If your daughter's relationship with her boyfriend doesn't feel right to you," he says, "then your willingness to intervene less frequently on little things like an unclean room can keep you in communication with her. As a result, your daughter may be willing to reach out to you to talk about big stuff, like her safety."

Accountability, Not Excuses: Intervention Strategies with Teen Boys

As discussed earlier in this chapter, boys are often taught by their parents, teachers, pastors, fellow church members, and society in general to conform to unhealthy characteristics. Males are taught never to cry, never to reveal any of their emotions except for anger, to use physical force and other forms of violence to get what they want, and to use females to meet their own sexual and emotional needs. And yet people still wonder why so many boys and men are violent. Let us read the story of one former teenage perpetrator of relationship violence.

David Garcia's Story

"I remember dating a girl when I was fourteen whom I really cared about," says David Garcia, a former batterer who is now a certified domestic violence counselor. "One of the things we'd do was sneak out of school at lunchtime and go to the Dairy Queen. My girlfriend didn't really like cutting classes. But no matter what she said, I always coerced her to do what I told her. I never said, 'Hey, you wanna go to Dairy Queen?' I'd demand that we go. I was very manipulative, always using people around me. I would also flirt with other girls to upset my girlfriend, so that we could get into a confrontation and I would have justification to be upset with her."

David was living out the same characteristics and tactics he had witnessed his father use against his mother. But as a young teen he was not aware of this dynamic. "Back then, I just remember telling my mom I was never going to be like my dad," he said. Then one day David used physical force against his own girlfriend.

"I remember we were arguing at her mother's house and she called me a fag," David says. "And I got really upset and slapped her. She looked really shocked, and I felt physically sick. My stomach started to hurt—as it would when my father was abusing my mother—and I went into the restroom and threw up. I knew that violence wasn't a healthy way to deal with problems. So I knew what I had done was wrong. However, thanks to my father, I was also aware that violence and other forms of abuse were ways males threaten females to get what they want. So there was obviously conflict inside me."

Feeling depressed, David began to engage in risky behavior. "A few times I even mutilated my body. And I started drinking heavily and smoking a lot of marijuana. I didn't want to be around anybody, and I stopped doing all schoolwork. By the time I came to second semester of eighth grade, I actually had no school credits at all. I was really depressed."

Because of his father's violence, at age four David and his siblings moved with their mother into Interval House Crisis Shelters in Long Beach, California. The agency serves abused women and their children living in Los Angeles and Orange Counties. "My father had been very physically and emotionally abusive to my mom and to us kids," David says. "In addition, he was an alcoholic and a womanizer, often bringing his girlfriends to our home. He was also a very jealous man who constantly accused my mom of having affairs with other guys. There were many times we had to run out of the house to neighbors because my dad threatened to teach my mom a 'lesson.' This lesson always ended with him beating and cussing at her."

Memories of these violent years flooded David's mind after he physically abused his girlfriend at age fourteen. "I was doing everything my father had done to us, everything I said I'd never do," the young man sighed. "As a result, I felt both ill and evil."

Around the same period of time, a national television talk show was planning a segment on domestic violence and its effects upon children who witness or experience abuse. The producers invited

David to be a guest on the show. "They wanted me to share my story about growing up at Interval House," David recalled. "The producers had no idea what I'd been doing in my life, and how I had perpetrated abuse against most of my girlfriends. I felt like a big hypocrite and didn't want to go on the show."

David says his mother and the other people at Interval House quickly figured out why he was so reluctant to go on national television. The young man then confessed his sins. "I thought they all would hate me," he admitted, "but instead they said 'David, we don't hate you. Let us help you.' The folks at Interval House were there for me. I got into batterers' intervention counseling and it helped a lot."

Nowadays, David uses his past—both the violence he witnessed and experienced as a little boy and the abuse he perpetrated against girls during his teenage years—to benefit other young people. "I'm a co-coordinator of the Second Generation, a program created a few years ago by Interval House. What I do is help other young people do drama therapy. We use acting as a therapy tool, dramatizing different situations that teens might have experienced growing up in homes where domestic violence was happening. Or the teens might also be involved in a violent dating relationship."

David and his Second Generation colleagues from Interval House travel around the state of California to educate people on teen dating and teen relationship violence intervention, as well as on adult intimate partner abuse awareness. The troupe performs regularly in churches and at schools. They also have spoken in front of the California State Legislature. In addition, the Police Officers Standard Training has used the Second Generation in training sessions.

David sees his counseling work as a calling. "My mission is to help young people and adults understand the effects domestic violence and teen relationship violence have on the entire family," he says. "It's the only time in my life I've been able to use my experiences to help other people. It helps me a lot, too. I'm still learning and still growing. I'm very fortunate to be able to use that which I thought was something to be ashamed of—my childhood—to help others. I know what I'm doing is making a difference. It's helped me to turn a negative into a positive."

Despite his outlook, David still carries the burden of all that he witnessed and experienced while growing up, and he still struggles with his spirituality. "I remember my mom taking us kids to church when we were little," he says. "And she'd be kneeling and praying and always crying. I used to wonder why God wasn't protecting her. Mom would tell us God loves and cares about us as his own children. So I kept wondering why God allowed so much violence to occur in our home. It didn't make any sense to me, and I found myself angry at God. At some point, I began to think there was no God. If he existed, I reasoned, then why did my family have to suffer so much?"

David's relationship with God remains ambivalent. The young man longs for the peace he sees in his mother. "Faith in God has really helped my mom a lot," he says. "She is one of the strongest people I've ever met, and my greatest role model. The peace of God has always been there for her. I want this same peace in my life, but have yet to grasp it. I guess you can say I'm still in process, still searching."

David's story offers many lessons. Christians who wish to help young men stop abusing their female intimate partners must learn these lessons in order to effectively use intervention strategies.

David's story reveals a solemn truth: Boys who grow up witnessing violence or experiencing abuse in their homes are at higher risk than other males to repeat this inappropriate behavior as teenagers and adults. If your son fits into this category, consider getting him help from the people who are trained in offender-specific interventions. (Although they mean well, youth ministers and pastors usually are not qualified to provide this type of help.) It is important to remember, however, that not all boys who grew up in violent homes go on to repeat these offenses, and some boys who grew up in loving and nonabusive homes abuse their teenage and adult intimate partners. Avoid guesswork about which boys or young men may be involved in abusive relationships. Personal history should be backed by evidence, and evidence should not be ignored in favor of an individual's "clean" personal history.

We also learn from David's story that we must hold perpetrators (in both teen and adult relationships) accountable for their sins while continuing to show them our compassion. The response offered to David by the people serving Interval House Crisis Shelters provides an ideal model for clergy, pastoral ministers, and parishioners to follow. When David disclosed his abusive past, the staff at the agency replied with compassion and concern. "David, we don't hate you," they said. "Let us help you." Perpetrators need help, not hatred, but must also be held accountable for the harm their behavior causes other people.

Regarding this last point, many Christians fall short. We recognize violence is wrong. But, as mentioned earlier, followers of Christ share the tendency of contemporary society to excuse or justify male-perpetrated abuse and violence. This is especially true when the offenses are perpetrated against women and girls and the accused men and boys are from our own congregation and community. Many Christians find it much easier to blame females for their own victimization than to face the harsh and messy truth that some boys and men who "praise" Jesus Christ and God also beat, cuss, rape, stalk, and abuse their girlfriends and wives.

Excuses and justifications will not draw abusive teenage boys from their violent ways. Our inaction will guarantee only that another generation of females will live in emotional, physical, psychological, sexual, and spiritual terror. Holding males accountable for the abuse and violence they perpetrate is our only hope to stop the cycle of male violence that has destroyed countless families through the ages.

David Garcia's experience also demonstrates that we must deal with the spiritual care of victimizers. Even though David and all other males who perpetrate intimate partner abuse have to be held accountable for their behavior, these boys and men also need our spiritual support to assist them in getting the help they require.

Christian clergy and laity can offer prayer and Scripture study that focuses on teachings that speak against violence and in favor of the equality, love, and respect that God and Christ offer to females as well as males. For example, these words of the apostle Paul are appropriate for study:

> For in Christ Jesus you are all children of God through faith. As many of you as were baptized into Christ have clothed yourself with Christ. There is no longer Jew or Greek, there is no longer slave or free, there is no longer male and female; for all of you are one in Christ Jesus (Gal. 3:26–28).

We can also provide perpetrators the encouragement to seek and stay in batterers' programs so that these young men can become nonabusive and nonviolent members of society.

Remember, never offer excuses or justifications for the violence males perpetrate against females or males. Also, resist the temptation to accept the often-recited proclamation by male perpetrators that they've been dramatically "changed by God." And avoid giving batterers trite solutions to their complex problems. For example, telling a batterer that all he needs to do to change is read the Bible, pray, seek forgiveness, and start attending church will not be helpful to him.

As David Garcia's experience illustrates, perpetrators can indeed turn their lives around. The road to lasting change can be an especially long and bumpy one, but with hard work and a willingness to commit themselves to programs designed to help batterers, these boys and men can change. Christians must hold out our hope for perpetrating boys and men and include them in our daily prayers. The words of Paul Kivel are as fitting for men, the population he examines, as for boys, and for Christians as much as society in general:

> Individual men who are violent need our support to make positive changes. Support should not be confused with collusion; the violent situation cannot be allowed to continue. Support must be conditional on the violence stopping.

To support a violent man we must:

- confront his violence;
- separate his violence from his worth as a person;
- help him understand that his violence comes from his hurt, pain, and powerlessness;
- help him see that violence is dangerous, self-defeating, and ineffective in getting his needs met;
- make a commitment to caring for him over time, providing a compassionate and empathetic ear to his experiences of violence, hostility, anger, and despair;
- recognize his training to be male and his unique place in the power hierarchies of our society, including those based on class, race, sexual orientation, and cultural background;
- help him understand that violence is learned and an unnecessary behavior that can be changed;
- address that part of the man that does not want to be violent and that does not want to hurt others;
- help him admit he has a problem;
- help him ask for help—perhaps one of the hardest things for a man to do.[4]

The Practice of Prevention and Intervention

Throughout this chapter we have indicated the various methods of prevention and strategies for intervention in situations of teen dating and teen relationship violence. Christians can take an important role in helping to care for both the teenage girls who are being victimized and the teenage boys who are perpetrating this sin. In summary, here are several concerns for us to keep in mind.

Put safety first. Safety must always be the number one priority in any violence prevention and violence intervention strategy. Nothing and no one should be placed before the goal of safety for everyone. Paul Kivel points out:

> Intervention is never easy. In a society in which interpersonal violence is taken for granted, it is risky for us to get involved—as if

we weren't already involved, as if we didn't already lead lives of fear because of the prevailing levels of violence. Next time it could be one of us who needs help. . . . Nevertheless, when interacting with violent men, we must remember that safety comes first! We must be safe from immediate danger and retaliation before we can ask someone to accept responsibility for his violence or offer support to him.[5]

Practice the team approach. Never attempt to prevent or intervene alone in situations involving teen dating or teen relationship violence. These are complex issues requiring a team of people from various disciplines.

Know your limits. Caring for victimized teenage girls, and for the boys who victimize them, is complicated work. Christians must never go beyond their level of expertise and training. Otherwise, we could severely compromise the safety of the teen victim, her family and friends, and ourselves.

Start early and repeat often. We must begin violence prevention education for our daughters and sons early, when they are still infants. We must teach our daughters and sons that they are unique and valued individuals. Our children must constantly hear from us that they should never force anyone, or be forced, to do anything that compromises their principles. And we must teach our children that no one deserves to be abused, under any circumstances.

Don't blame the victim. No one can cause another person to use violence. A man's decision to use violence has nothing to do with what a woman does, says, wears, etc. This behavior is always chosen by the person perpetrating it. He is fully responsible for his behavior. Therefore, Christians must never suggest that a teenage girl is to blame for the abusive and violent actions of a teenage boy. She never causes him to beat, curse, rape, stalk, or violate her in any other way. Never.

Hold perpetrators accountable. Even if a teenage boy grew up in a violent home, even if he is angry at someone or something for the unjust way he has been treated, he has no right to use violence against another person (or pet, property, etc.). When a young man chooses to abuse or violate someone else (yes, he is making a *choice* to do this), he must be held accountable for his sinful actions. Christians must never make excuses or offer justifications for the violence males perpetrate.

Pray for and offer hope to both survivors and perpetrators. Christians have a responsibility to care for the people who are being violated *and* for those individuals who victimize others. We must reach out to both groups. In all cases, however, we must avoid offering quick-fix solutions or trite statements of "comfort" that ultimately do more harm than good.

Conclusion

How are we members of the body of Christ working to prevent violence and intervene in situations of violence that occur among our teenage daughters and sons? Denying that the problem exists in our homes, communities, and congregations will not cause teen dating and teen relationship violence to decrease. Excusing and justifying abusive and violent behavior perpetrated by our teenage sons, and blaming our teenage daughters for their own victimization, won't help matters either.

Our children are in danger. Millions of our daughters are being abused emotionally, physically, and sexually each year by millions of our sons. The problem exists as much among Christian young people—attending our churches, youth fellowships, and Christian schools—as it does among young people in the overall population.

What are we, as members of the body of Christ, going to do about teen dating and teen relationship violence? If we are to provide effective and sensitive care to our sons and our daughters, we must first acknowledge that the problem exists among us. We must be willing to seek the necessary education and training to help us gain a better understanding of these issues. We must be willing to teach our daughters and our sons, from a very early age and on a regular basis, that no one ever deserves to be abused, and that violence, under any circumstance, is always wrong. And we must impress upon our boys and girls the fact that they are loved, respected, and viewed as equals in the eyes of God and Jesus Christ.

Questions for Discussion

1. What violence prevention and violence intervention programs are in place in the congregation where you worship? If there are none, why is that the case? What might be done to change that?
2. Name and discuss at least five lessons Barbara Chandler has taught her son, Bryant, about violence prevention.
3. Are teenage girls being victimized by teenage boys in your congregation? If you answer no, why do you think this widespread problem is not present in your church? If you answer yes, what are members of the congregation doing about these incidents?
4. Name and discuss the three unhealthy lessons talked about in the chapter that are taught to boys. Which, if any, of these lessons have you taught your own sons?
5. Name and discuss three reasons why victimized teenage girls are reluctant to disclose the abuse to their parents and other adults.
6. Describe your feelings after reading David Garcia's story. How would you help this young man deal with his spirituality?
7. Are you and your adult intimate partner modeling for your children mutual equality, love, and respect? Are you also modeling healthy responses to the conflicts you and your adult intimate partner face from time to time? Elaborate.

5.

Working as Partners

Throughout this book, we have talked about the need for Christian clergy and laity to seek education and training *before* trying to aid survivors and perpetrators of dating violence and intimate partner abuse. We also have discussed some of the dangers, to would-be helpers as well as victims and their families, in addressing these complicated problems alone or without sufficient preparation and expertise. To be most effective, Christian caregivers need the assistance of community service providers: advocates, batterers' intervention specialists, child protective services providers, crises intervention counselors, law enforcement officers, legal professionals, shelter workers, and victim and witness assistance personnel, to name just a few.

Christians' efforts to address these complex issues without proper training and assistance from experts can be compared to me, a hospital chaplain, attempting to perform surgery on patients who come to the medical center. I am educated and trained to offer patients and their families spiritual and emotional care. It is a very important role. However, I cannot do the work of a neurosurgeon, anesthesiologist, or surgical nurse. I am not qualified to do these jobs and should not even try them.

"Clergy and laity need to know very clearly what is and what is not their role," cautions the Rev. Dr. Anne Marie Hunter, a United Methodist minister and founder of the Safe Havens Interfaith Partnership against Domestic Violence in Boston. The agency provides the religious community advocacy and education on the issue of domestic violence and trains religious people to help in concert with service providers within the community.

Hunter speaks of the perils of Christians going beyond their limits. "It can be dangerous to victims and helpers, for example, for Christians to shelter someone at a home or church parsonage without support and training from a battered women's service provider," she says. "It can be dangerous to victims and helpers for Christians to confront a batterer or try to be the batterer's intervention counselor. It can be dangerous to victims and helpers when Christians try to settle a domestic violence situation themselves rather than working with the police and the courts. It can be dangerous to victims and helpers for Christians to respond to crises by going to the house themselves rather than asking the victim for permission to call the police on the victim's behalf."

Why aren't more clergy and laity from Christian denominations creating partnerships to deal better with situations of domestic violence? Are there any successful partnerships, whether among Christian groups or between Christian congregations and community domestic violence service providers? What are the key components of successful collaborative efforts? How can we as a Christian community urge more of our clergy members to address the global problem of violence against women and children? We will focus our attention in this final chapter on these important questions.

Obstacles to Partnerships

Historically, there has been a great deal of distrust between domestic violence service providers and the Christian community. Service providers fear (not without justification, as we have seen) that ordained ministers and congregation members will pressure or force abused women to stay in dangerous and unhealthy marriages and cite Bible passages to justify their viewpoint. Also, service providers express concern that churchgoers will blame women for their own victimization.

On the other hand, pastors and parishioners suspect that many community domestic violence service providers encourage battered women to seek divorce from abusive husbands, thus breaking the sacred covenant of marriage. Others fear that such providers will teach Christian women "humanism," or try to "convert" Christian women to lesbianism, or cause Christian women to "lose their faith" by espousing "worldly views." Let us take a closer look at what battered women are hearing from community service providers and members of the Christian community.

Responses from Community Service Providers

I have never heard a community domestic violence service provider encourage an abused woman to divorce her abusive husband. Nor has any survivor ever reported to me that a service provider instructed her, against her will, to dissolve her marriage. (Because ordained ministers and church members express this concern at nearly all the domestic violence prevention trainings I conduct, I now ask conference attendees if they themselves have ever heard of a community service provider counseling a battered woman to get a divorce. To date, no one has cited a confirmed case of this occurring.)

Several battered Christian women have, however, mentioned concerns about the responses they've received from community service providers about their religious beliefs and practices. Expressing guilt for taking their children and themselves away from abusive husbands (even though the women recognize the need for safety), survivors say they tell secular counselors and shelter workers that the Bible, their church, and their pastors "demand" women to submit to the "authority of their husbands." Therefore, the victims say, they believe they must never divorce their husbands and must return home to them as soon as possible.

In response, some service providers tell the abused women, "Don't worry about what the Bible or your church and pastor tell you. Safety for you and your children needs to be your number-one concern!" Although I agree that safety for victims and their children must be the top priority of any domestic violence prevention and intervention strategy, I also believe it is never appropriate for anyone to tell a survivor not to worry about her religious beliefs and practices.

In truth, most abused women who are Christian will be concerned about what the Bible, the church, and their pastors think about what they do and say. Thus, it is not helpful for community domestic violence service providers, or anyone else, to tell survivors not to worry about these important aspects of their faith. "Battered religious women come with some challenging therapeutic needs that have both sacred and secular overtones," writes Nancy Nason-Clark, an author and university professor who has studied the effects of domestic violence on women from the Christian faith for a number of years.

> Having the violence condemned by their spiritual leader has a powerful impact on the life of a religious woman, an effect that cannot normally be replicated in a social work office or the local shelter. Too often, women are advised by secular workers, wary of clerical or religious advice, to abandon their faith journey in the search for healing and wholeness. Many agency counselors feel handicapped in their ability to work with religious victims whose values they perceive to be in conflict with certain treatment options.[1]

In an ideal partnership, community domestic violence service providers who feel ill-equipped to address the beliefs and values of a Christian battered woman would seek the assistance of trained members of the survivor's faith community. A clergy person or congregation member trained in domestic violence intervention and possessing an understanding of the victim's beliefs and values could be of tremendous help to the survivor. However, as we'll see, many churchgoers are not prepared to meet abused women's religious and spiritual needs.

Responses from Christian Communities

"If pastors or lay members are not prepared to work with community service providers, then they are not prepared to respond to the needs of a survivor," says the Rev. Dr. Anne Marie Hunter. Despite this warning from a longtime expert on the effects of domestic violence on religious women, many Christians are very reluctant to make referrals to, or partner with, community service providers.

Spiritual leaders and congregants who attempt to work alone with an abused woman or who try to provide care without proper training place the woman, her children, and themselves in tremendous danger. This fact cannot be over-emphasized. No one person can take on all the roles needed to give a battered woman and her children the best hope for safety. Even experts with extensive background and training are not qualified to work alone with victims and perpetrators. It is of great concern that many of the ordained ministers who attend my talks readily admit they have little or no training in domestic violence prevention and intervention, yet they counsel victims and perpetrators.

Pastors' and churchgoers' inappropriate responses to adult intimate partner abuse are numerous and well-chronicled. As a result of these responses, community service providers have been slow to trust members of the faith community when it comes to offering effective and sensitive care to battered women. "In the early days of the domestic violence assistance movement, women coming into shelters very often told stories of how the church blocked their exit from an abusive situation," recalls Mary Walton, a pioneer in the movement who works as the clinical director consultant for Interval House Crisis Shelters in Los Angeles and Orange Counties. Walton, the daughter of a Christian minister, is also a certified candidate for ordained ministry in the United Methodist Church.

"Churches have historically not been interested in having families separate, not even for the purpose of a woman's safety," Walton says. "Instead, churches have been far more interested in keeping families intact, in order to ensure that families will be in church. And the structure of the family unit has been clearly defined by the faith community: husband, wife, and children, all under the leadership of the husband." Walton explains how a traditional view of family put forth by some religious communities has alienated the church from the community of domestic violence service providers. "The patriarchal view of a woman's role—in the family, parish, and in the community—is a very dangerous position for women and children. And the fact that the church has not often spoken out on the violence men perpetrate against women and children places the institution in direct conflict with members of the domestic violence assistance movement. Unlike the church, our number-one priority has always been to provide safety for women and children."

For more than seven years, Cathy Hartle has worked as executive director of the Hands of Hope Resource Center, which serves abused women and children in two rural counties of central Minnesota. Hartle vividly recalls a situation involving a battered woman who sought help from her spiritual leader. "This woman went to her pastor and told him how her husband had been physically abusing her," Hartle says. "Well, the pastor told the woman to go home and fulfill her duty as a Christian wife, and to work harder at making her marriage successful. The pastor then told the husband everything the wife had shared. This ensured two things: first, that the wife would receive at least one more beating from her husband. And second, that the wife would never go to her pastor for help again."

Cyndi Anderson also serves battered women and children in rural Minnesota. For the past eleven years she has been the director of Lakes Crises Center in Detroit Lakes, a community in northwestern Minnesota. Anderson is also troubled by the number of stories she's heard abused Christian women tell about members of the faith community.

"I believe most people want to help victimized women," Anderson says. "But I think one of the most destructive things pastors and parishioners do when they learn of a situation of domestic violence is to suggest that the wife go with her abusive husband to marriage counseling. Church members just don't seem to understand why this type of referral doesn't work and how it places victims in greater danger."

Anderson is also disturbed by the stories that abused women tell about ordained ministers and lay people using Scripture to justify a man's violent behavior. In one such incident, she says, "A Christian woman came into our office with one side of her face very bruised. The victim's husband had broken her jaw. This abused woman said she was shocked over what her husband had done, but was even more stunned by the response of her male pastor. The minister first told his battered parishioner that she needed to be a better wife. As awful as this response was, the woman said she could tolerate it—until the pastor told her that the Bible 'required' her to 'turn the other cheek.' It was simply awful advice to give to anyone—especially to a woman whose husband had just broken her jaw."

There is clearly a major difference between the responses offered by community service providers and by members of the Christian community. Community service providers generally tend to believe an abused woman's story, and they immediately offer her various avenues of safety. Christian clergy and lay members generally tend to blame a battered woman for her own victimization and express that the top priority is to keep the family together regardless of the danger this poses to a victim and her children. These differences must be overcome if victims of intimate partner abuse are to receive comprehensive help from their communities.

Obstacles to Christians Working Together

Partnerships between community domestic violence service providers and the faith community occur far too infrequently. It is also rare for Christians to join together—within an individual congregation or in church clusters—to work toward ending abuse and violence among couples. Why? Let us look at three of many reasons: complacency, denial, and reluctance on the part of clergy to get involved.

Complacency

"As Christians, we need to get up off our backsides and look after our sisters and brothers who need help," Jim Croucher says. Recall from chapter 3 that his daughter, Tina, was murdered by her boyfriend in 1992 (see pages 84-87). Jim believes the complacency many people of faith reveal when it comes to relationship violence and abuse is wrapped up in the notion that Christians are somehow protected from the problems of the world. "We all must face the harsh fact that being a Christian certainly doesn't exempt us from social ills," he says. "When it comes to situations of domestic violence and teen dating violence, victims and perpetrators are everywhere—even in our own neighborhoods and in our own churches. We have to get involved in the care of our own because, as Christians, we not only make a commitment to God but also a commitment to help one another."

In her groundbreaking book *Woman-Battering,* Carol J. Adams warns Christians about the dangers of being a bystander:

> Naming the violence, ensuring safety, and creating accountability do not take place in a vacuum, but occur within the midst of community. For many women who suffer violence, and for the men who hurt them, the church is a vital, if not major, source of community experiences. It may respond negatively, shunning and stigmatizing the battered woman and the battering man. The church community may think it is taking a neutral stance in response to the problem of woman-battering, but neutrality results in ignoring or dismissing the problem. . . . Bystanders, by their nature, side

with the perpetrators by allowing violence to go unchallenged. The alternative is for the church community to determine that it will enhance the positive environment for naming and accountability that you are creating in your ministry.[2]

Complacency on the part of Christian ordained ministers and lay people can exacerbate the pain and sorrow suffered by abused Christian women and teenage girls. "There wasn't anybody from the church that helped me or my mom," says Christie Corpuz, who was abused by her Christian father as a young girl and her Christian boyfriend during her teenage years. "The pastor knew that my father was abusive to Mom and me. But he told my mother, 'It's better to have a bad husband and father than no husband and father at all.' From this pastor's words, I got the impression that it's better to have a husband and father who beats the hell out of you, than to not have a man around the house at all!"

Christie, now in her twenties, is deeply troubled that most congregation members extended no care to her and her mother. "Pastors and other Christians at our church didn't help us because, I think, they didn't know how," Christie says. "Everyone kept telling us that God is our comfort and strength. But then they'd turn around and blame us for the abuse we were experiencing from my violent father, often quoting scriptures to support their claims. I realize that a lot of Christians gave these responses because they didn't know what else to do. But I'm still very hurt by the way they treated my mom and me. If Christian clergy and parishioners don't know how to help victims, then doing nothing is certainly not the answer. Instead, they need to get the proper education and training in domestic violence awareness so that they can be of help."

Denial

I had lived in Hawaii for less than a month when one of the managers at the medical center where I serve as chaplain referred "Amy," a twenty-five-year-old local woman, to me. Though Amy was not a hospital employee, the manager referred her anyway, saying that Amy would benefit from the support of a "pastor with an accurate biblical perspective." The manager offered no further explanation of her statement, saying that her meaning would be clear once I had met Amy. I agreed to see the young woman.

Beautiful in mind and spirit, Amy radiated confidence, grace, and vitality. After ten minutes of small talk, I asked her why she had decided to see me. "I got married eight months ago," she explained, the glow on her face quickly receding into a shroud of sadness. "My husband, Samuel, who's really a great Christian guy that everyone loves, has not been himself lately. For the past several weeks, he, uh, has, uh, been under a lot of pressure at work. And sometimes . . . sometimes, he, he, uh, says and does things to me that he later feels awful about. As I've said, we're both long-standing Christians, so I just know, pastor, I know. . . ."

Amy's words trailed off as she began to cry. I watched in silence, not wanting to interrupt what appeared to be a very deep expression of pain and sorrow. When her tears began to subside several moments later, I asked her to say more about what her husband did and said to her when he felt "under pressure." Describing herself as a "mediocre cook at best," Amy said she understood why Samuel had told her the week before that the dishes she prepared weren't "fit for a starving rat." The young woman also seemed to accept the reason her husband had recently called her a "stupid bitch": because she had forgotten to buy the type of bagels he liked. Amy even expressed understanding why Samuel had begun referring to her as a "cold fish" and a "sexual retard." After all, she explained, "men need sex more often than women."

I told Amy that no one deserved to be criticized or referred to with such emotionally and sexually abusive language, and that Samuel's actions were in clear violation of how the Christian Scriptures instruct husbands to treat their wives. Then I asked Amy if she had discussed this situation with her pastor.

Tears welled in Amy's eyes. She told me that my colleague at the medical center, who knew both Amy and Samuel from church, had suggested she meet with me because of the way their own ordained minister had responded to Amy's disclosure.

"I thought I could tell Pastor Ralph what was happening in my marriage without his taking sides. After all, he's known both Samuel and me since we were teens, and he also officiated at our wedding."

But Amy discovered that her assumption was inaccurate. "Pastor Ralph said, 'Samuel certainly doesn't look or act like a person who would say such things, Amy. He's a fine Christian young man. I just can't imagine him ever saying the horrible things you're accusing him of saying. Is this a particularly emotional time of the month for you?'" Amy had left Pastor Ralph's office feeling depressed and sickened, knowing that the clergy person was blaming her for Samuel's behavior.[3]

Pastor Ralph's response demonstrates the common expression of denial victims often encounter when they disclose abuse to pastors and other members of their congregations. As discussed earlier, many pastors and churchgoers harbor stereotypical profiles of abusive men. They believe that perpetrators of abuse come from nonwhite racial groups, have no religious affiliation, abuse alcohol and other drugs, are poor, uneducated, and, if employed at all, are blue-collar workers. In short, they simply deny and believe that "perpetrators are not to be found in our congregation."

Many perpetrators of domestic abuse in fact *do* fit into one or more of the above categories. Many others, however, are white, middle or upper classes, and faithful churchgoers; they hold degrees in education, law, medicine, theology; they serve their communities as attorneys, physicians, professional athletes, university professors, and pastors.[4]

When we deny that Christian men and boys violate their wives and girlfriends, we do a great injustice to victimized women and girls. Refusal to face the truth reinforces churchgoers' belief that they can blame abused women for the violence they suffer. Denial also makes it impossible for us to lead male perpetrators to the help they need.

Perpetrators of domestic abuse cannot be identified by the manner in which they present themselves in public. They are often charming and master manipulators. They attract a vast amount of praise from people who know them outside their homes. "Carl is a wonderful Christian, husband, and father. He gives a lot of money and most of his free time to the work of the church." "Mike is such a great guy, visiting ill and elderly persons at nearby hospitals and retirement centers." "Samuel is a fine Christian young man, an excellent youth worker, and a loving husband to his beautiful young wife, Amy."[5] We Christians must be guided by a discerning spirit, not denial. Victims and perpetrators of intimate partner abuse are everywhere—including in our communities and congregations.

Pastors' Reluctance to Get Involved

Clergy involvement is essential to congregations' effectiveness at addressing the violence perpetrated against the women and children of their communities. "We find that both clergy and laity involvement is crucial if the congregation is going to move forward on this issue," the Rev. Dr. Anne Marie Hunter says. Later in this chapter we will learn more about her agency's efforts to educate and train clergy and lay members in domestic violence awareness. "The entire congregation needs to make a serious commitment. When we train only clergy, they begin to respond differently to domestic violence, but then they may get pressure from lay members who say, 'this is not how it's been done in the past.' Similarly, we find that if only the laity are trained they will try to go forward with the domestic violence program, but without clergy support they are not able to engage the congregation, so the program doesn't get the support it needs."

Having an ordained minister name domestic violence for what it is—criminal and sinful behavior—from the pulpit, in the classroom, at board meetings, during times of prayer, and while attending violence prevention marches, rallies, vigils, and workshops, sends a powerful message to the entire faith community. "If our spiritual leader cares enough to be involved," parishioners might infer, "then we also want to participate." A second message clergy participation sends to members of the congregation and community is deeply personal: victimized women get the strong sense that their spiritual leader is a safe person, and their congregation a safe place, to begin to disclose the horrors that are occurring in their homes.

Unfortunately, many ordained ministers—women as well as men—are reluctant to get involved in issues surrounding abuse and violence in the homes of their parishioners. When I conduct domestic violence trainings for the religious community, clergy are, by far, the group least represented. Even when a symposium is planned months in advance, even when conference organizers clear the date of an event with spiritual leaders *prior* to scheduling it, even when the seminar is being held at the pastor's own church, few clergy show up! Why?

In my first book, *Domestic Violence: What Every Pastor Needs to Know,* I sought answers to this troubling phenomenon. In a series of interviews with Catholic and Protestant ordained ministers serving in various areas of the United States, five consistent themes arose: Clergy are reluctant to get involved in situations of adult intimate partner abuse owing to denial; a sense of fear and helplessness; a lack of appropriate training; sexist attitudes; and the fact that some of our male clergy are themselves perpetrators of domestic abuse.[6]

Education and training tools that address intimate partner abuse are readily available in articles and books, on videos and the Internet, and at conferences, but many clergy members refuse to take advantage of these golden opportunities to learn. Some spiritual leaders continue to cling to the false belief that no Christian man or boy would violate his female intimate partner. Other clergy, while recognizing the global and pervasive nature of domestic violence, choose to ignore the problem when it occurs among couples in their congregations because it is messy and uncomfortable. And, sad to say, we must face the fact that some of our male pastors harbor misogynist and sexist views, and/or perpetrate domestic violence themselves. These men believe that, as males, they have a right to do whatever they desire with their wives, girlfriends, and all other females.

The picture is grim, but certainly not hopeless. Although we will never get all spiritual leaders to appreciate the vital role they can take in helping to prevent and eradicate domestic violence, there are many clergy who will, with our gentle prodding, become involved in the struggle against these issues.

Helping More Clergy Become Involved [7]

I arrived at my office one morning a few years ago and discovered, strategically placed in front of the computer on my desk, a copy of the video *Broken Vows*. Produced by the Center for the Prevention of Sexual and Domestic Violence in Seattle, the video offers religious perspectives on adult intimate partner abuse. Affixed to the front of the tape was a handwritten note: "Al, I look forward to discussing this video with you in a few days." The individual who left the message was one of the chaplain residents assigned to the medical center where I serve as head of the hospital ministry department. An astute and energetic young woman, the resident was diligent in her mission to help clergy and other pastoral ministers become involved in the care of victims and their dependent children.

Even though I had previously viewed *Broken Vows* and was already encouraging other spiritual leaders to do the same, I greatly appreciated the resident's efforts. Because so many clergy members are reluctant to get involved in the issue of domestic violence, those of us who have been trained—whether we are ordained ministers, Christian lay people, or serve the community in some other capacity—need to be creative and nonthreatening in our approach. How then can we help more spiritual leaders become effectively involved in both the care of victims and in holding perpetrators responsible for their crimes? Here are a few approaches to consider.

Impress upon clergy their important and unique role in caring for victims. The emotional and spiritual support clergy can offer abused women is crucial to the well being of these women. Christian victims often seek the assistance of clergy and other Christians first—before going to secular agencies—because they are struggling with such spiritual concerns as the Christian understanding of divorce, forgiveness, and the roles of men and women in a marriage. Clergy members who have been trained in domestic violence response must impress upon our less-informed colleagues that with proper education they, too, can be of tremendous help to battered women.

Invite clergy members and other pastoral ministers to attend, with you, classes, workshops, and ministerial retreats in which the topic of domestic violence is addressed. The key words in the preceding sentence are *with you.* Denial, complacency, fear and helplessness, and the lack of proper education and training decrease the likelihood that reluctant ministers will attend sessions about domestic violence on their own.

I have found it helpful to invite clergy colleagues in the context of discussion about why it is important *for me* to attend a particular domestic violence conference. This takes the focus off the other clergy member. Rather than risk making a colleague feel that you believe he or she has inadequate knowledge of the topic, convey the invitation in a way that is more collegial and community-minded: "I'm going to attend this seminar on domestic violence. You know, it's such a complicated issue that I find I need to frequently take a refresher course to make sure I'm providing abused women the most effective emotional and spiritual care I can offer. Why don't you join me? Afterward, let's discuss ways we can work together to better serve victims in our community."

Congregation members should also feel free to suggest to their ordained ministers that training in domestic violence awareness is in the best interest of the community. Ministers, after all, are leaders who serve—they serve God and their congregations—and input from congregants regarding the community's needs is relevant and should be welcomed.

Discuss with ordained ministers articles, books, and videos on domestic violence. Print and video resources can be very helpful in causing spiritual leaders to become appropriately involved in caring for abused women and in holding perpetrators accountable for their actions. As with conferences and workshops, it is best to take a nonthreatening, invitational approach to introducing these materials to ministers. The chaplain resident who left *Broken Vows* on my desk was wise and creative. She did not simply give me the video and leave it at that, nor did she try to coerce or "guilt" me into viewing it. She brought it to my attention in a casual way and included a friendly invitation for us to review the material together. This approach makes it less likely that a disinclined spiritual leader will put the item aside and forget about it.

Personalize the problem of violence against women. Ask spiritual leaders, gently but directly, to imagine that their own daughters or beloved nieces are being beaten, raped, stalked, and violated by an intimate or former intimate male partner. Then inquire of these same ordained ministers how they would help their abused and battered daughters or nieces. I guarantee this approach will compel many more clergypeople to seek education and training in domestic violence response.

Working Together

In the final section of this chapter, we will consider three stories. Each focuses on the positive steps Christian clergy and laity are taking toward ending violence against women and children in their congregations and communities. The people who share their stories recognize the importance of working together with other Christians and with community domestic violence service providers. The stories are not panaceas, nor do they promote unrealistic expectations and outcomes. Those interviewed speak candidly about what does and does not work in their situations. I thank each participant for her or his willingness to share. From these stories may all of us take seeds to plant in our own congregations and communities.

Citizens against Domestic Violence

"About six months after Tina was murdered, Elsa and I were in counseling," Jim Croucher recalls, "and one of the counselors suggested that we try to make something good happen from this tragedy by helping other people." That particular conversation ended then and there. The Crouchers were so completely devastated by their daughter's murder that, according to Jim, they could not consider the counselor's advice. But four years later, the grieving parents began to ponder the recommendation. "We really felt called to do something," Jim says, "to help other people in the name of Tina. We had to somehow turn our daughter's useless and senseless death into something that could keep another girl from being murdered."

In 1996, Elsa and Jim Croucher started Citizens against Domestic Violence (CADV). Comprehensive Counseling Service, a nonprofit state-certified mental health and chemical dependency treatment provider in Middletown, Ohio, helped launch the CADV program. The presence of a variety of professionals on CADV's board reflects the commitment of a diverse community. It includes several ordained ministers from the various Christian denominations in the area, several retired schoolteachers, a nurse, a police chief, a domestic violence court advocate, a domestic violence counselor, the executive director of Comprehensive Counseling Service, and Elsa and Jim Croucher.

The task of CADV is a model of partnerships among community members represented by the board members. Jim says, "What we do here in Middletown and the surrounding areas is join together as a group of concerned citizens, all of us trained by community domestic violence service providers, to offer emergency assistance for victimized women and their children. We can place a victim into a safe haven on a moment's notice, twenty-four hours a day, seven days a week. While a victim is in our safe haven, we offer her food, lodging, and safety. We give her time to put together her thoughts on what she wants to do next. And, if the victim gives us permission, we also bring in our domestic violence counselor and court advocate. These two community service providers can offer a victim further legal options."

Middletown's faith community also plays an important role in CADV. However, as Jim warns, Christian clergy and laity need to know their limits. "At our domestic violence talks with church groups, Elsa and I always remind our sisters and brothers of faith that we must not act as though we're a domestic violence counselor, a court advocate, the police, or a shelter worker, or act as anyone trained to offer batterers treatment," Jim says. "However, we do tell other Christians that with proper training in domestic violence awareness, they can listen to, offer prayers for, and be a friend to a victim. Still, we impress upon churchgoers the need to set limits. We are not qualified to counsel victims and perpetrators, we always remind people at our talks. This complicated role needs to be handed over to experts in the community."

Jim is equally clear that the organization has no intention of ever putting religious beliefs, teachings, and traditions ahead of the safety of a victimized woman and her children. "It's not CADV's intent to break up a family, but it is our intent to keep every family member safe," he says. "We are instruments of God, and with God's guidance we think we might be able to help victims and their children. We tell members of our Christian family all the time that they too can assist the people who are dealing with situations of teen dating and domestic violence. But, as we always point out, the greatest assistance all Christians can provide is to help victims get to safety."

Safe Havens Interfaith Partnership against Domestic Violence

Safe Havens Interfaith Partnership against Domestic Violence began in 1991 in Boston, Massachusetts. "Our organization does various things," says executive director and founder the Rev. Dr. Anne Marie Hunter, "but they all fall under the rubric of advocacy and education within the religious community. We're particularly concerned about and focused on safety for victims and accountability for batterers."

In 1998, Safe Havens launched a program called the Family Violence Prevention Project. Says Hunter, "This program offers twenty-two hours of training to congregations on domestic violence awareness during the course of the academic year. And we require all participating congregations to send a team of people to the training. This team must involve both clergy and laity. We also strongly encourage the congregations to put teams in place that include laity from the various aspects of the life of the congregation; for example, someone from education, someone from the women's group, someone from the men's group, someone from the social justice group. We try to encourage congregations to have a team that involves the entire working body of the church, including worship."

Safe Havens's training is faith-based. During the twenty-two hours, the sessions cover such issues as: the dynamics of domestic violence; how to hold batterers accountable; how to work with local domestic violence service providers; the impact of domestic violence on young children and youth; teen dating violence; sexual assault, especially within the context of marriage; the barriers to leaving a violent relationship; and traumatization, self-care, and healing.

An essential aspect of the training is to help congregation members understand the importance of partnerships with community service providers. "We find sometimes when clergy and laity are wanting to respond to situations involving domestic violence that they attempt to be the police, the courts, the shelters, and everything else," Hunter says. "So what we are attempting to promote is a community-wide response that will allow the police to do what they do, the courts to do what they do, the shelters to do what they do, and the emergency room personnel to do what they do."

Hunter also hopes that the training will help clergy and laity to better understand their crucial role in the care of domestic violence victims and perpetrators. "The religious community has a very important role in early intervention and prevention of violence. Clergy and laity are also gateways to referrals when they provide individual pastoral counseling for victims and support for batterers as they seek help from a battered women's service provider and a batterers' intervention program. The religious community can also take a key role in referring children in violent homes to services for children who have witnessed or been part of domestic violence."

Every aspect of the Safe Havens training encourages clergy and laity to work in partnership with service providers. "We train all our participants in how to make referrals to community service providers, how to work with them, and how to know enough about the basics of domestic violence to be able to help victims access these services," Hunter says. "We also train clergy and laity to respond effectively to faith issues. When members of the religious community are able to listen, respond to the faith crises, and make appropriate referrals, family members get the help they need."

The Rev. Lorraine Thornhill, pastor of the First Holiness Church in Cambridge, Massachusetts, participated with four members of her congregation in the Safe Havens training. "During the training, presenters talked about how some Christian husbands justify the abuse they perpetrate against their wives by claiming male headship," Thornhill says. "This was new information for me. I already knew that women have always been looked upon as second-class citizens, even in the church. But men using Scripture to beat and abuse their wives in many other ways? This was really an eye-opener! The training helped me to become more aware of this sad reality. As a result, nowadays I spend a lot more time in my sermons addressing the issue of domestic violence. I tell members of the congregation that there is no justification, biblical or otherwise, for men to use abuse or violence against their wives and girlfriends. None!"

Thornhill describes other changes she and her congregation have made after the Safe Havens training. "We now display two posters that speak against domestic violence. This is significant because we never before put up posters in our church." Placed in well-trafficked areas of the church building, the posters offer victimized women information on how they can get help for themselves and their children. "At the bottom of each poster is a tear sheet with a number to call," Thornhill says. "No one knows who takes this information, so safety and anonymity of victims is maintained."

Thornhill and the rest of the trained team have begun presenting what they learned about domestic violence to those people who lead other ministries in the congregation. The team is planning a formal training for all church leaders in the near future. "The response has been good, especially because we've already been discussing the issue of domestic violence with folks on an individual basis," Thornhill says. "In fact, many leaders are asking us 'When are we going to have the domestic violence training?' This is a very positive sign."

Whenever that training does take place, Thornhill says she will most surely invite community service providers to participate. "One of the many good things that has grown out of the Safe Havens training is that our team became enlightened on the role of community service providers in response to situations of domestic violence. When my team and I were being trained, the police, a person from the district attorney's office, a shelter worker, and many other experts from the community talked with us. They spoke about the variety of services available to women, men, and children in our area. This was really helpful."

Learning about the work of other professionals serving the Boston area was not the only lesson Thornhill learned. The community domestic violence service providers also helped to dispel some of her preconceived notions. "The stereotype I had about service providers was that they wouldn't be willing to come talk with church folk," the faith leader confesses. "But at the Safe Havens training, my team and I quickly realized the opposite is true. The service providers gave us a bunch of their cards and tons of helpful information. Then they told us they'd come back whenever invited. Their kind and open response has caused me to change my attitude. This is what I now tell people in my church, and other clergy throughout our community: 'We all need to know about domestic violence. It's an issue inside and outside the church. There are people from the community we can call for help. They are more than willing to come meet with us at any time. We need to take advantage of their expertise. As Christians, all of us need to get involved.'"

Creating a Safe Environment

Historically, the African American community and the faith community have not had easy access to the resources available for abused women and their children. "The Rev. Cherrye Cunnigan and I presented a few events together during Domestic Violence Awareness Month [October]," recalls Mary Walton, a pioneer in the domestic violence assistance movement and longtime Christian. "We wanted to reach the underserved group of African Americans and the underserved group of church folk. So we put together a worship service and sponsored a concert. Then along the way came the opportunity for funding, which allowed us to provide assistance to these underserved communities in a more ongoing fashion."

February 1, 2000, marked the official start of a partnership between Interval House Crisis Shelters, the agency Mary Walton serves as clinical director consultant, and Zaferia Shalom Zone Agency, the outreach agency at Wesley United Methodist Church, where Cherrye Cunnigan serves as pastor. Located in Long Beach, California, their joint project is called Creating a Safe Environment (CASE). One of CASE's primary goals is to promote knowledge of domestic violence resources among the faith community and African American families in the greater Long Beach area. Cunnigan and Walton, both of whom are African American, serve as CASE's project directors.

"The African American community is very patriarchal," Cunnigan says. "In this patriarchal community, women who are committed Christians who are living in marriages where they are subjected to violence and abuse many times find that violence and abuse reinforced by their male pastors. For instance, the pastor will often say such things as 'God will not give you more than you can bear.' A female who has just been abused, maybe even the night before, and who is now sitting in the congregation hearing her pastor say that will not feel supported."

Cunnigan also discusses how the patriarchal system in the African American community can prevent male clergy members from holding Christian men accountable for their abuse. "Many times the abuser has a high profile and is well-respected by leaders in the congregation," she says. "And the leaders are so invested in the male parishioner that they choose not to see, and they don't want to hear, that this man may be abusing his wife. The faith leaders don't want to even enter that possibility into their equation. As a result, many church women in the African American community suffer in silence. The women actually end up believing that they themselves are doing God some kind of service by staying in an unhealthy and abusive marriage. Meanwhile, their children are being subjected to the atrocities of abuse. Many of these kids grow up to repeat the horrible cycle they learned at home. And yet, people continue to wonder 'Why is there so much violence in African American communities?'"

Out of a deep concern for the well-being of African American families in general and at-risk African American women and children in particular, CASE made the education of the faith community in domestic violence assistance one of its top priorities. Cunnigan and Walton thought the best way to reach this population would be African American clergy. "We had it all planned out in our heads," Walton says. "Interval House would take care of issues and concerns related to community service and formal education about domestic violence. And Zaferia would address clergy and invite them into the process. It would just have that affinity, we told ourselves. We were very naive. Pastor Cunnigan and I had certainly expected some resistance from the clergy. But we never thought we'd get the degree of resistance we received and the way it manifested itself."

One of the biggest issues was sexism. CASE is managed by women. Most of the ordained clergy in the Long Beach and surrounding areas are men. "The whole undertone from male clergy was 'What is it that you women want?'" Walton says. "Those words were never openly spoken, but there was tension and envy and greed on the part of members of that group—not from all the clergy, but in different corners this type of attitude began to rear its ugly head. My personal analysis of the situation was that because the church is so dominated at the top by male leadership, many of the pastors from those denominations were not open to forging bridges and collaborations and cooperative situations with shelters and domestic violence assistance programs where there are primarily women in leadership positions."

Both Walton and Cunnigan identified an all-day domestic violence conference sponsored by CASE in January 2001 as the event that began to turn the attitude of African American male clergy in the Long Beach area in a more positive direction. "That particular event made a tremendous difference in terms of the clergy's receptivity to the information we have access to," Walton says, "and also in the willingness of the ordained ministers to want to work with us. What helped most, I think, was the fact that we brought in a male African American ordained minister to be our resource person. That day generated excitement and strong interest. Afterward, the clergy even asked us to put together a forty-hour domestic violence training for them."

One specific breakout session had a particularly strong impact. During this ninety-minute meeting, the African American male clergy spent time alone with the invited speaker. "In the wisdom of the Holy Spirit," Cunnigan says, "we were able to do that ninety-minute session. It turned out to be the most powerful event of the entire day. When the session was scheduled to end, I remember knocking on the door of the room to see if it was okay for me to enter. And all these male voices replied, 'No, no, no, we're not finished! Don't come in yet!' The session went on another half hour."

I had the privilege of taking part in the domestic violence conference just described. I have also had the pleasure of returning to Long Beach to follow up with both community service providers and some of the African American clergy and lay leaders who attended the all-day event. The CASE partnership is in full bloom and making a huge difference in the lives of churchgoing African American women, children, and men. Not only are ordained ministers receiving necessary training, but so are church lay members. "We realized that even though we might have the attention of the clergy and their respect and leadership, we also needed the lay people in the congregation involved," Cunnigan says. "Without the lay people doing the follow-up, a large piece would be missing. There's only so much a pastor can do on a regular basis, and there are some things going on in the congregation that the pastor does not even know about. So lay people are a vital part of this partnership."

As stated earlier, these projects in Ohio, Massachusetts, and California offer no panacea or easy answers. Mary Walton points out, "Bridging the gap between community service providers and members of the faith community around the issue of domestic violence is not always a smooth process. But it is a process nonetheless." I believe it is unrealistic for any of us to think that the long history of tension between community service providers and members of the Christian community will suddenly become resolved simply because of one well-received domestic violence conference in Long Beach or in any other location.

Nevertheless, teaming together provides our best hope for preventing and intervening in situations of adult intimate partner abuse and teen dating and teen relationship violence. As members of the Christian faith community and as service providers working in various roles, we must put aside our long held assumptions, bigotry, fears, myths, resistance, and stereotypes about each other and join together. Otherwise, victimized women and children will suffer even more injustice.

Conclusion

Where do we go from here as a Christian community? We can continue to deny the occurrence of domestic abuse and teen dating and teen relationship violence in our neighborhoods and congregations. We can choose not to work side by side with individuals especially trained to deal with victimized females and with the males who abuse them. These choices, however, will perpetuate myths that have devastated Christian women and children for centuries. They will put women, children, and our communities at great risk.

Where will we go from here as a Christian community? Throughout this book, we reviewed alternatives to the all-too-common choices made by Christian communities. Whatever our decision, it is important to always remember that our actions and inactions greatly affect the safety and security of our mothers, our children, our sisters, and many other people dear to us.

Questions for Discussion

1. Name and discuss five factors behind the long history of tension between the Christian community and community domestic violence service providers. As a Christian, do you harbor certain stereotypes about community service providers? Specify.

2. Name the three obstacles discussed in this chapter that block Christians from working together to end adult intimate partner abuse. Have any of these obstacles been an issue for you personally? Which ones?

3. What did you feel as you read about the abuse Amy suffered at the hands of her Christian husband, Samuel? Why do you think Pastor Ralph responded as he did? How would you respond to Amy's disclosure of abuse? Elaborate.

4. Do the pastors in your church speak out against intimate partner abuse? If the answer is yes, give specific details on how these issues are being addressed (for example, in sermons, classrooms, during congregational prayers, etc.). If the answer is no, why do you think the pastors are not addressing these concerns?

5. Name and discuss at least four approaches parishioners can take to help more clergy become involved in the care of victims and perpetrators. What approaches have you tried? How did your pastor respond to your efforts?

6. Name at least three positive lessons you learned from the collaborative efforts of people in Ohio, Massachusetts, and California. How would your own congregation respond to suggestions of partnering with community service providers?

7. What are you, as a concerned Christian, now going to do about the situations of adult intimate partner abuse and teen dating and teen relationship violence occurring in your own congregation and community?

Appendix A:
Selected Resources

Books

Adams, Carol J. *Woman-Battering*. Minneapolis: Fortress Press, 1994.

Adams, Carol J., and Marie M. Fortune, eds. *Violence against Women and Children: A Christian Theological Sourcebook*. New York: Continuum, 1995.

Betancourt, Marian. *What to Do When Love Turns Violent: A Practical Resource for Women in Abusive Relationships*. New York: HarperCollins, 1997.

Borg, Marcus J. *The God We Never Knew: Beyond Dogmatic Religion to a More Authentic Contemporary Faith*. San Francisco: HarperSanFrancisco, 1997.

Borg, Marcus J. *Reading the Bible Again for the First Time*. San Francisco: HarperSanFrancisco, 2001.

Bussert, Joy M. K. *Battered Women: From a Theology of Suffering to an Ethic of Empowerment*. New York: Division for Mission in North America, Lutheran Church of America, 1986.

Cooper-White, Pamela. *The Cry of Tamar: Violence against Women and the Church's Response*. Minneapolis: Augsburg Fortress, 1995.

DeYoung, Curtiss Paul. *Reconciliation: Our Greatest Challenge—Our Only Hope.* Valley Forge, Pa.: Judson Press, 1997.

Dobash, Emerson R., and Russell Dobash. *Violence against Wives.* New York: The Free Press, 1979.

Dutton, Donald G. *The Abusive Personality: Violence and Control in Intimate Relationships.* New York: Guilford Press, 1998.

Fortune, Marie M. *Keeping the Faith: Questions and Answers for the Abused Woman.* San Francisco: HarperSanFrancisco, 1987.

Gaddis, Patricia Riddle. *Battered but Not Broken: Help for Abused Wives and Their Church Families.* Valley Forge, Pa.: Judson Press, 1996.

Hull, Gretchen Gaebelein. *Equal to Serve.* Grand Rapids, Mich.: Baker Books, 1987.

Jacobson, Neil, and John Gottman. *When Men Batter Women: New Insights into Ending Abusive Relationships.* New York: Simon and Schuster, 1998.

Keener, Craig S. . . . *And Marries Another: Divorce and Remarriage in the Teachings of the New Testament.* Peabody, Mass.: Hendrickson, 1991.

Kivel, Paul. *Men's Work: How to Stop the Violence That Tears Our Lives Apart.* Center City, Minn.: Hazelden, 1992.

Kroeger, Catherine Clark, et al., eds. *Study Bible for Women: The New Testament.* Grand Rapids, Mich.: Baker Books, 1995.

Kroeger, Catherine Clark, and James R. Beck, eds. *Healing the Hurting: Giving Hope and Help to Abused Women.* Grand Rapids, Mich.: Baker Books, 1998.

Kroeger, Catherine Clark, and James R. Beck, eds. *Women, Abuse, and the Bible: How Scripture Can Be Used to Hurt or Heal.* Grand Rapids, Mich.: Baker Books, 1996.

Kroeger, Catherine Clark, and Nancy Nason-Clark. *No Place for Abuse: Biblical & Practical Resources to Counteract Domestic Violence.* Downers Grove, Ill.: InterVarsity Press, 2001.

Levy, Barrie. *Dating Violence: Young Women in Danger.* Seattle: Seal Press, 1991.

Levy, Barrie. *In Love and in Danger: A Teen's Guide to Breaking Free of Abusive Relationships.* Seattle: Seal Press, 1998.

McDill, S. R., and Linda McDill. *Dangerous Marriage: Breaking the Cycle of Domestic Violence.* Grand Rapids, Mich.: Fleming H. Revell, 1991.

Miedzian, Myriam. *Boys Will Be Boys: Breaking the Link between Masculinity and Violence.* New York: Anchor Books, 1991.

Miles, Al. *Domestic Violence: What Every Pastor Needs to Know.* Minneapolis: Fortress Press, 2000.

Miller, Mary Susan. *No Visible Wounds: Identifying Nonphysical Abuse of Women by Their Men.* New York: Fawcett Columbine, 1995.

Mowat, Barbara A. and Paul Werstine, eds. *The Tragedy of King Lear* by William Shakespeare. New York: Pocket Books, 1993.

Murray, Jill. *But I Love Him: Protecting Your Teen Daughter from Controlling, Abusive Dating Relationships.* New York: HarperCollins, 2000.

Nason-Clark, Nancy. *The Battered Wife: How Christians Confront Family Violence.* Louisville: Westminster John Knox Press, 1997.

Pipher, Mary. *Reviving Ophelia: Saving the Selves of Adolescent Girls.* New York: Ballentine Books, 1994.

Pollack, William S. *Real Boys' Voices.* New York: Random House, 2000.

Rashkow, Ilona. *Taboo or Not Taboo: Sexuality and Family in the Hebrew Bible.* Minneapolis: Fortress Press, 2000.

Ruether, Rosemary Radford. *Women-Church: Theology and Practice.* New York: HarperCollins, 1985.

Stangler, Mary. *Striving to be . . . Violence Free: A Guidebook for Creating a Safety Plan.* St. Louis Park, Minn.: Perspectives, Inc., 1995.

Torjesen, Karen Jo. *When Women Were Priests: Women's Leadership in the Early Church and the Scandal of their Subordination in the Rise of Christianity.* New York: HarperCollins, 1993.

Trible, Phyllis. *Texts of Terror: Literary-Feminist Readings of Biblical Narratives.* Philadelphia: Fortress Press, 1984.

Walker, Lenore E. *The Battered Woman.* New York: Harper and Row, 1979

Walker, Lenore E. *The Battered Woman Syndrome* (Rev. ed.). New York: Springer, 2000.

Weems, Renita J. *Battered Love: Marriage, Sex, and Violence in the Hebrew Prophets.* Minneapolis: Fortress Press, 1995

Videos

The following educational videos, produced by the Center for the Prevention of Sexual and Domestic Violence in Seattle, Washington, are invaluable resources for training clergy, laity, seminary faculty, students, and the staff of shelters and domestic violence programs. (For more information call the Center at 206-634-1903; or visit their Web site at www.cpsdv.org):

Broken Vows: Religious Perspectives on Domestic Violence. A videotape series in two parts, *Broken Vows* is intended for clergy, congregations, religious educators, and staff of shelters and domestic violence programs.

Love—All That and More. A three-video series featuring teens talking with teens about healthy relationships. Designed to inform youth about the elements that make up healthy relationships, and increase their awareness and understanding about abuse; it offers adults a window into the often private world of teens, and seeks to motivate all viewers to seek relationships based on equality and mutual respect.

Wings Like a Dove: Healing for the Abused Christian Woman. A thirty-four-minute videotape, intended for abused Christian women. It is designed to use in battered women's shelters, churches, fellowship meetings, and other settings where women come together.

Appendix B:
State Coalitions, Internet
Resources, and Organizations

State Coalitions

Alabama Coalition against Domestic Violence—Montgomery, Alabama,
Phone: 334-832-4842

Alaska Network on Domestic Violence and Sexual Assault—Juneau, Alaska,
Phone: 907-586-3650

Arizona Coalition against Domestic Violence—Phoenix, Arizona,
Phone: 602-279-2900

Arkansas Coalition against Violence to Women & Children—North Little Rock,
Arkansas, Phone: 501-812-0571

California Alliance against Domestic Violence—Sacramento, California,
Phone: 916-444-7163

Statewide California Coalition for Battered Women—Van Nuys, California,
Phone: 562-981-1202

Colorado Coalition against Domestic Violence—Denver, Colorado,
  Phone: 303-831-9632
Connecticut Coalition against Domestic Violence—East Hartford, Connecticut,
  Phone: 860-282-7899
Delaware Coalition against Domestic Violence—Wilmington, Delaware,
  Phone: 302-658-2958
District of Columbia Coalition against Domestic Violence—Washington, D. C.,
  Phone: 202-783-5332
Florida Coalition against Domestic Violence—Tallahassee, Florida,
  Phone: 850-425-2749
Georgia Coalition against Domestic Violence—Atlanta, Georgia,
  Phone: 404-209-0280
Hawaii State Coalition against Domestic Violence—Aiea, Hawaii,
  Phone: 808-486-5072
Idaho Coalition against Sexual and Domestic Violence—Boise, Idaho,
  Phone: 208-384-0419
Illinois Coalition against Domestic Violence—Springfield, Illinois,
  Phone: 217-789-2830
Indiana Coalition against Domestic Violence—Indianapolis, Indiana,
  Phone: 317-543-3908
Iowa Coalition against Domestic Violence—Des Moines, Iowa,
  Phone: 515-244-8028
Kansas Coalition against Sexual & Domestic Violence—Topeka, Kansas,
  Phone: 785-232-9784
Kentucky Domestic Violence Association—Frankfort, Kentucky,
  Phone: 502-695-2444
Louisiana Coalition against Domestic Violence—Baton Rouge, Louisiana,
  Phone: 225-752-1296
Maine Coalition for Family Crisis Services—Bangor, Maine,
  Phone: 207-941-1194
Maryland Network against Domestic Violence—Bowie, Maryland,
  Phone: 301-352-4574
Massachusetts Coalition of Battered Women's Service Group—Boston,
  Massachusetts, Phone: 617-248-0922
Michigan Coalition against Domestic Violence—Okemos, Michigan,
  Phone: 517-347-7000
Minnesota Coalition for Battered Women—St. Paul, Minnesota,
  Phone: 651-646-6177
Mississippi Coalition against Domestic Violence—Jackson, Mississippi,
  Phone: 601-981-9196
Missouri Coalition against Domestic Violence—Jefferson City, Missouri,
  Phone: 573-634-4161
Montana Coalition against Domestic Violence—Helena, Montana,
  Phone: 406-443-7794

Nebraska Domestic Violence and Sexual Assault Coalition—Lincoln, Nebraska, Phone: 402-476-6256

Nevada Network against Domestic Violence—Reno, Nevada, Phone: 775-828-1115

New Hampshire Coalition against Domestic and Sexual Violence—Concord, New Hampshire, Phone: 603-224-8893

New Jersey Coalition for Battered Women—Trenton, New Jersey, Phone: 609-584-8107

New Mexico Coalition against Domestic Violence—Albuquerque, New Mexico, Phone: 505-246-9240

New York State Coalition against Domestic Violence—Albany, New York, Phone: 518-432-4864

North Carolina Coalition against Domestic Violence—Durham, North Carolina, Phone: 919-956-9124

North Dakota Council on Abused Women's Services—Bismarck, North Dakota, Phone: 701-255-6240

Action Ohio Coalition for Battered Women—Columbus, Ohio, Phone: 614-221-1255

Ohio Domestic Violence Network—Columbus, Ohio, Phone: 614-784-0023

Oklahoma Coalition on Domestic Violence & Sexual Assault—Oklahoma City, Oklahoma, Phone: 405-848-1815

Oregon Coalition against Domestic and Sexual Violence—Salem, Oregon, Phone: 503-365-9644

Pennsylvania Coalition against Domestic Violence—Harrisburg, Pennsylvania, Phone: 717-545-6400

(Puerto Rico) Commission Para Los Asuntos de a Mujer—Santurce, Puerto Rico, Phone: 787-722-2907

Rhode Island Council on Domestic Violence—Warwick, Rhode Island, Phone: 401-467-9940

South Carolina Coalition against Domestic Violence & Sexual Assault— Columbia, South Carolina, Phone: 803-256-2900

South Dakota Coalition against Domestic Violence & Sexual Assault—Pierre, South Dakota, Phone: 605-945-0869

Tennessee Task Force against Domestic Violence—Nashville, Tennessee, Phone: 615-386-9406

Texas Council on Family Violence—Austin, Texas, Phone: 512-794-1133

Utah Domestic Violence Advisory Council—Salt Lake City, Utah, Phone: 801-538-9886

Vermont Network against Domestic Violence and Sexual Assault—Montpelier, Vermont, Phone: 802-223-1302

Women's Coalition of St. Croix, Virgin Islands—St. Croix, Virgin Islands, Phone: 340-773-9272

Virginians against Domestic Violence—Williamsburg, Virginia,
   Phone: 757-221-0990
Washington State Coalition against Domestic Violence—Olympia, Washington,
   Phone: 360-407-0756
West Virginia Coalition against Domestic Violence—Charleston, West Virginia,
   Phone: 304-965-3552
Wisconsin Coalition against Domestic Violence—Madison, Wisconsin,
   Phone: 608-255-0539
Wyoming Coalition against Domestic Violence and Sexual Assault—Laramie,
   Wyoming, Phone: 307-755-5481

Internet Resources

Keyword: domestic violence. Many links to information, support groups, books,
and organizations specializing in adult intimate partner abuse and teen dating and
teen relationship violence prevention and intervention.

Organizations

Center for the Prevention of Sexual and Domestic Violence
An interreligious, educational resource
2400 North 45th Street, Suite 10
Seattle, Washington 98103
Phone: 206-634-1903
Fax: 206-634-0115
E-mail: cpsdv@cpsdv.org
Web site: www.cpsdv.org

National Coalition against Domestic Violence
National Office
P.O. Box 18749
Denver, Colorado 80218-0749
Phone: 303-839-1852
Fax: 303-831-9251
Web site: www.ncadv.org

National Domestic Violence Hotline: 800-799-SAFE (800-799-7233)
A 24-hour referral service for domestic violence shelters and therapists
specializing in the treatment of abusive relationships.

Notes

Introduction

1. American Medical Association, "Facts about Domestic Violence." Available on-line at www.ama-assn.org/ama/pub/category/4867.html, accessed August 11, 2001.

Chapter 1

1. American Medical Association, "Facts about Domestic Violence." Available on-line at www.ama-assn.org/ama/pub/category/4867.html, accessed August 11, 2001.
2. Domestic Abuse Project of Delaware County, "Here are some things you should know about domestic violence . . ." Available on-line at www.libertynet.org/~dapdc/, accessed August 14, 2001.
3. American Medical Association, "Facts about Domestic Violence." Available on-line at www.ama-assn.org/ama/pub/category/4867.html, accessed August 11, 2001.
4. National Institute of Justice, "Intimate Partner Violence Is Examined in New Justice Department Report." Available on-line at www.ojp.usdoj.gov/pressreleases/2000/nij00141.htm, accessed April 13, 2001.

5. A portion of Rachel Leah Boer's story is told in Al Miles's, *Domestic Violence: What Every Pastor Needs to Know* (Minneapolis: Fortress Press, 2000), pp. 95-99.

6. L. Kevin Hamberger and Clare Guse, "What Domestically Violent Men Say about Their Partners' Violence" (unpublished), pp. 1-2.

7. Developed by Dr. Anne L. Ganley for the Family Violence Prevention Fund, 1995.

8. A portion of this story is told in Al Miles, "Domestic Violence: Helping More Clergy Become Involved in the Care of Victims," *The Clergy Journal*, August 2000, pp. 37-38.

9. Al Miles, "When Words Abuse," *Leadership*, Spring 1999, p. 98.

10. From Sheila Y. Moore, "Adolescent Boys Are the Underserved Victims of Domestic Violence," *Boston Globe*, Dec. 26, 1999, p. E7, quoted in *No Place for Abuse*, Catherine Clark Kroeger and Nancy Nason-Clark, (Downers Grove, Ill.: InterVarsity Press, 2001), p. 83.

11. See Miles, "When Words Abuse," p. 99.

12. Ibid., p. 100.

13. Neil Jacobson and John Gottman, *When Men Batter Women* (New York: Simon and Schuster, 1998), p. 214.

14. See Miles, "Domestic Violence: Helping More Clergy Become Involved in the Care of Victims," p. 40.

The author extends a warm *mahalo* to Terry Boer, Allana Wade Coffee, Christie Corpuz, L. Kevin Hamberger, Kim Smith King, Janine Limas, Mark-Peter Lundquist, Carol Miles Underwood, "Anita," "Gladys," "Margaret," "Leslie," and "Sandy" for their willingness to be interviewed for this chapter.

Chapter 2

1. Tertullian, *On the Dress of Women* 1,1, in *Anti-Nicene Fathers*, vol. 4, eds. James Donaldson and Alexander Roberts (New York: Scribners, 1899), p. 14. Quoted in Rosemary Radford Ruether, *Women-Church: Theology and Practice* (New York: HarperCollins, 1985), pp. 137-138.

2. Augustine, On the Trinity 7,7,10; in *Later Works*, ed. John Burnaby (Philadelphia: Westminster Press, 1955). Quoted in Ruether, p. 138.

3. Thomas Aquinas, *Summa Theologica* pt. 1, q. 92, art. 1; ed. Anton Pegis (New York: Random House, 1945). Quoted in Ruether, p. 138.

4. *Malleus Maleficarum*, pt. 2, sec. 6; trans. *Montague Summers* (London: J.Rodker, 1928). Quoted in Ruether, pp. 138-139.

5. Martin Luther, *Lectures on Genesis*, Gen. 2:18, in *Luther's Works* vol. 1, ed. Jaroslav Pelikan (St. Louis: Concordia Publishing House, 1958), p. 115. Quoted in Ruether, p. 139.

6. Karl Barth, *Church Dogmatics*, vol. 3, sec. 4 (Edinburgh: Clark, 1975), pp. 158-72. Quoted in Ruether, p. 139.

7. *Declaration on the Question of the Admission of Women to the Ministerial Priesthood*, sec. 27. (Vatican City, October 15, 1976). Quoted in Ruether, p. 139.

8. A portion of this story is told in Al Miles, "A Perpetrator? Can't Be!," *The Clergy Journal*, January 2000, p. 37.

9. Catherine Clark Kroeger and Nancy Nason-Clark, *No Place for Abuse* (Downers Grove, Ill:. InterVarsity Press, 2001), p. 104.

10. Ibid., pp. 146-147.

11. Marie M. Fortune, *Keeping the Faith: Guidance for Christian Women Facing Abuse* (San Francisco: HarperCollins, 1987), p. 37.
12. "Introduction to the Book of Malachi," from the Holy Bible, New International Version, International Bible Society, p. 1487.
13. See Kroeger and Nason-Clark, *No Place for Abuse,* 131-132.
14. Catherine Clark Kroeger, "God's Purposes in the Midst of Human Sin," in *Women, Abuse, and the Bible,* eds. Catherine Clark Kroeger and James R. Beck (Grand Rapids, Mich.: Baker Books, 1996), p. 207.
15. Catherine Clark Kroeger, "The Classical Concept of 'Head' as 'Source,'" in Gretchen Gaebelein Hull, *Equal to Serve* (Grand Rapids, Mich.: Baker Books, 1987), p. 278.
16. David M. Scholer, "The Evangelical Debate over Biblical 'Headship,'" in *Women, Abuse, and the Bible,* p. 43.
17. See Kroeger in Hull, *Equal to Serve,* p. 282.
18. Catherine Clark Kroeger, "Let's Look Again at the Biblical Concept of Submission," in *Violence against Women and Children,* eds. Carol J. Adams and Marie M. Fortune (New York: Continuum, 1995), p. 136.
19. See Miles, *Domestic Violence: What Every Pastor Needs to Know,* p. 133.
20. Ibid., p. 148.
21. William Shakespeare, *The Tragedy of King Lear.* Barbara A. Mowat and Paul Werstine, eds. (New York: Pocket Books, 1993), p. 223.
22. See Miles, *Domestic Violence: What Every Pastor Needs to Know,* p. 147.
23. Marie M. Fortune, "Forgiveness: The Last Step," in *Violence against Women and Children,* p. 206.

The author extends a warm *mahalo* to Kim Smith King, Janine Limas, Mark-Peter Lundquist, "Anita," "Gladys," "Lani," "Leslie," and "Paula" for their willingness to be interviewed for this chapter.

Chapter 3

1. Jill Murray, *But I Love Him: Protecting Your Teen Daughter from Controlling, Abusive Dating Relationships* (New York: HarperCollins, 2000), p. 7.
2. Ibid.
3. Ibid., p. 23.
4. Ibid., pp. 24-25.
5. Ibid., p. 53.
6. Al Miles, "Anger at God after a Loved One Dies," *The American Journal of Nursing,* March 1998, pp. 64-66.

The author extends a warm *mahalo* to Jerry Coffee, Christie Corpuz, Elsa Croucher, Jim Croucher, Michael Fukuda, David Garcia, Rodney Kahao, Barrie Levy, "Lorena," and "Brenda" for their willingness to be interviewed for this chapter.

Chapter 4

1. Paul Kivel, *Men's Work: How to Stop the Violence That Tears Our Lives Apart* (Center City, Minn.: Hazelden, 1992), p. 236.
2. Carole Sousa, "The Dating Violence Intervention Project," in *Dating Violence: Young Women in Danger,* ed. Barrie Levy (Seattle: Seal Press, 1991), pp. 228-229.

3. Jill Murray, *But I Love Him: Protecting Your Teen Daughter from Controlling, Abusive Dating Relationships* (New York: HarperCollins, 2000), p. 117.

4. See Kivel, *Men's Work,* p. 152.

5. Ibid., p. 151.

The author extends a warm *mahalo* to Bryant Chandler, Barbara Chandler, Jerry Coffee, Christie Corpuz, David Garcia, Barrie Levy, and "Margaret" for their willingness to be interviewed for this chapter.

Chapter 5

1. Nancy Nason-Clark, "Making the Sacred Safe: Woman Abuse and Communities of Faith," *Sociology of Religion 2000,* p. 364.

2. Carol J. Adams, *Woman-Battering* (Minneapolis: Fortress Press, 1994), p. 115.

3. A portion of this story is told in Al Miles, "A Perpetrator? Can't Be!" *The Clergy Journal,* January 2000, p. 28.

4. Ibid., p. 37.

5. Ibid.

6. Al Miles, *Domestic Violence: What Every Pastor Needs to Know* (Minneapolis: Fortress Press, 2000), p. 166.

7. This material was first published in Al Miles, "Domestic Violence: Helping More Clergy Become Involved in the Care of Victims," *The Clergy Journal,* August 2000, pp. 37-40.

The author extends a warm *mahalo* to Cyndi Anderson, Christie Corpuz, Jim Croucher, Cherrye Cunnigan, Cathy Hartle, Anne Marie Hunter, Lorraine Thornhill, and Mary Walton for their willingness to be interviewed for this chapter.

*   *   *   *   *